Welcome to
The HISTORY of
FASHION

When Marie Antoinette married into the French royal family, she couldn't have foreseen the bloody, brutal end that she would meet at the guillotine. Instead, she was dazzled by the Bourbon bling, the splendour of her future home at the Palace of Versailles, and the ostentatious dresses worn by those living at the royal court. Like the queens that came before her, she embraced the excesses of her new life, notoriously buying 300 new dresses a year at a time when France was in financial turmoil. She might be considered a fashion icon by today's standards, but it's little wonder the people of France were repulsed by her at a time when they could barely afford bread.

In this brand-new title from the makers of All About History magazine, discover the remarkable story of fashion and how it evolved from a hand-sewn luxury embraced by the extremely wealthy and passed down through generations, to the mass-produced fast fashion that spills out of our wardrobes today. We'll delve into some of the deadliest fashion trends, and find out how wartime rationing changed the perception of womenswear for good.

CONTENTS

26
THE ART OF EMBROIDERY
Unravel the rich history and intricate artistry behind the timeless craft of embroidery

32
LOOKS TO DYE FOR
Colourful clothes for all is a fairly recent innovation. Before that, colourways were the ultimate in conspicuous consumption – and you could be punished for disobeying the style rules...

38
MARIE ANTOINETTE'S EXTREME MAKEOVER
The ill-fated queen of France's marital makeover is enough to give even the most committed bridezilla nightmares

44
HOW TO GET A BAROQUE HAIRSTYLE
Dress your hair in a coiffure that turns heads, just like the it-girls in Versailles

46
EAST MEETS WEST
Western fashion does not exist in a vacuum; for centuries it has been influenced by global culture and has, in turn, influenced other cultures too

52
DROP DEAD GORGEOUS
13 of history's most dangerous fashion trends

58
FASHION AND THE INDUSTRIAL REVOLUTION
The Industrial Revolution ushered in a whole new era of fashion, changing that rarefied world forever

6
20 ROYAL FASHION TRENDS
The sartorial crazes that swept around the world and the royal figures who helped to make them a sensation

12
FOR THE LOVE OF CODPIECES
When skirts, tights and frills were all the hallmarks of masculinity

18
HOW TO SEW AN ELIZABETHAN RUFF
Make your own Tudor fashion statement

20
BIGGER IS BETTER
Charting the evolution of European women's fashion through the Middle Ages and beyond

114

122

66

46

86
THE ROARING TWENTIES
As the world breathed again after war, fashion was undergoing its own revolution as it stepped out into the Jazz Age

94
EDWINA MOUNTBATTEN'S WEDDING DRESS
In keeping with the decade's latest sartorial style, Edwina Mountbatten's simple gown channelled flapper fashion

96
COURTING CONTROVERSY
The remarkable rise and dubious legacy of Coco Chanel

102
MAKE DO AND MEND
In WWII fashion was on the ration, but that didn't stop the ladies of Britain from finding ways to keep their wardrobes up to date, with a few pointers from the Ministry of Information

108
DIOR'S NEW LOOK
How Christian Dior's extravagant designs put the frill back into postwar fashion

112
QUEEN ELIZABETH II'S CORONATION ATTIRE
Discover the ornate outfit that Elizabeth II wore to her coronation ceremony

114
FASHION GOES FAST
The postwar technologies and economy of the 1960s saw a radical reimagining of how clothing was created, and who for – but it all started with an accident…

120
PRINCESS DIANA'S WEDDING DRESS
The secrets hidden in the seams of Diana's iconic dress

122
WHAT LIES BENEATH…
From going commando to drawers, corsets and a gentleman's linen, the history of underwear is a fascinating one

64
SPINNING JENNY
Inside the mechanism that revolutionised fashion

66
DEMURE LADIES
The real-life fashions of the Regency period

72
THE GREAT MASCULINE RENUNCIATION
The story of Beau Brummell and the birth of the suit

78
QUEEN VICTORIA'S WEDDING DRESS
There were many trends that were started during the reign of Queen Victoria, but the white wedding dress's popularity continues to soar to this day

80
THE UGLY GIRL PAPERS
A series of magazine articles in 1870s America aimed to help women avoid ugliness, and achieve beauty – at whatever the cost

84
THE TRIANGLE SHIRTWAIST FACTORY FIRE
Inside the 1911 tragedy that paved the way for safety in the workplace

72

05

20 ROYAL FASHION TRENDS

The sartorial crazes that swept around the world and the royal figures who helped to make them a sensation

Written by Jonathan Gordon

20 royal fashion trends

Before the age of style magazines and entire industries dedicated to clothing trends, many ambitious people looked to the world's most powerful figures and emulated their clothing decisions to curry favour. As mass media opened up these styles to wider public consumption, so the importance of royal fashion became of as much interest to the average person on the street as it had once been to courtiers. To this day, perhaps more as celebrities than as royals, those with a connection to the great dynasties of the world have huge sway over what clothes and looks are hot in the moment. Here, we'll take a look back at 20 examples of fashion trends kick-started by royal association.

WHITE WEDDING DRESS
Queen Victoria

When: 1840 **Where:** UK

The white wedding dress has become so traditional as to seem practically timeless, but prior to the marriage of Queen Victoria to Albert, Prince of Saxe-Coburg-Gotha, wedding dresses were not quite so uniform as they are today. A white dress, while not unheard of, was a rather impractical choice for most brides since the dress was likely to be worn more than once and keeping it pristine would be very challenging for all but the very rich. Queen Victoria wearing a white dress was therefore both a display of her wealth as well as helping her stand out at her ceremony. Paintings of the event spread around the globe, making the choice popular everywhere. It's worth noting that Victoria also chose a white dress to show off the Honiton lace work from Devon, an ailing industry in the region that suddenly exploded thanks to her patronage.

LONG WIGS
Louis XIII

When: 1624 **Where:** France

While his son would go down in history as the bigger fashion-icon, Louis XIII had a pretty significant contribution to make to the sartorial norms of the 17th century when he began to wear a wig. It all started with the king having long, natural hair in his youth, of which he was very proud. But as he began to go bald in his early 20s he turned to wearing a wig to maintain his image, and the court wasn't far behind him. In the years that followed, men wearing long wigs became the fashion in French high society and gradually began to disseminate through the lower stratas of the kingdom. The wearing of a wig began to infer social status and authority, in emulation of the king, and even merchants and street vendors might be expected to don a wig when dealing with the public.

PIE-CRUST COLLAR
Diana, Princess of Wales

When: 1980s **Where:** UK

Princess Diana's place as a style icon was more or less secured the moment she became a public figure, as is true of most royal women, but she had a fair few more fashion moments than most. From the 'revenge dress' to being the first royal woman to wear trousers to an official event, Diana was groundbreaking. Perhaps it will be surprising to learn, then, that probably her biggest fashion contribution was the humble pie-crust collar. A style that came out of the 1970s, but a favourite blouse style of Diana's in the early 80s, the pie-crust collar has more than a little of the classic ruff about it, evoking royal portraits of the 16th and 17th century. Thanks to the princess the collar became very popular, and is a style that keeps coming back into vogue to this day.

ROCOCO PIONEER

Madame de Pompadour

When: 1745
Where: France

As the mistress to Louis XIV, Madame de Pompadour (birth name Jeanne-Antoinette Poisson) sits slightly on the outskirts of royal acclaim, but her position made her just as influential as any blue-blooded princess. In particular her taste in floral, pastel dresses helped to push the Rococo style throughout the French court and to the wider European gentry in the mid-18th century.

KID'S SAILOR SUIT

Edward VII

When: 1846 **Where:** UK

When Albert Edward, Prince of Wales, stepped aboard the royal yacht in 1846 aged only four or five, he's unlikely to have expected his clothing would start a trend that stretches the world over even now. In actuality, while the future Edward VII was wearing the sailor suit that would become a phenomenon, it was Queen Victoria who made the choice for her son. She had commissioned the uniform from a navy tailor in the hopes of surprising her husband, Prince Albert, who loved it so much he had a painting ordered. Images of Edward in his outfit became incredibly popular, as did dressing up children in sailor outfits. In turn, the style started to be adopted as official school uniforms in some schools and began spreading across the empire. To this day, some schools in Japan still use a sailor outfit style for their uniforms.

CAT-EYE SUNGLASSES

Princess Margaret

When: 1950s **Where:** UK

An unquestionable fashion icon of her era, Princess Margaret was a pioneer among royal women with her sense of style that was more in keeping with a Hollywood star than a Windsor. And much like Audrey Hepburn and Elizabeth Taylor, her adoption of cat-eye sunglasses helped to propel the style into an international trend.

TARTAN

Queen Victoria

When: 1852 **Where:** UK

When King George IV crossed into Scotland in 1822 he was the first British king to do so since Charles II, starting a close bond between the royals and Scotland. Victoria and Albert's love of the country was exemplified by their adoption of tartan in clothing, even creating their own Balmoral Tartan that's still worn by British royals.

20 royal fashion trends

THE REBIRTH OF HAUTE COUTURE
Empress Eugénie of France
When: 1858 **Where:** France

While Marie Antoinette was pretty unpopular with the masses in her time (and for decades afterwards) there can be no denying her impact on French fashion, but the French Revolution put something of a pause on the excesses of the wealthy in France. By the mid-19th century tempers had cooled enough for Empress Eugénie, wife of Emperor Napoleon III, to pick up where her forebear had left off. Her right-hand man in this effort was Charles Frederick Worth, a designer from Lincolnshire, who worked with Eugénie to push daring new trends. First came massive skirts held up with crinoline, inspired by Marie Antoinette, then snug dresses with bustles. Each item was bespoke and handmade, helping to relaunch the French fashion industry and reignite the opulent haute couture styles that had fallen out of favour.

CHIN SCARF
Queen Louise of Prussia
When: 1797 **Where:** Prussia

While Louise of Mecklenburg-Strelitz died tragically young at the age of 34, she managed to start the rather remarkable fashion trend of wearing scarves under the chin. It appears to have started with various portraits and a statue by Johann Gottfried Schadow where she wore a scarf to cover a swelling. The unusual look caught on for a short time.

A TINY WAIST
Empress Elisabeth of Austria
When: 1865 **Where:** Austria

Empress Sisi was one of the great royal celebrities of her time, renowned for her stunning dresses, very long hair and a stringent exercise and dieting regime. In actuality, it's believed she suffered from anorexia, which would account for her tiny 50cm waist, made smaller still in a corset that set off a trend for extreme waistlines across Europe.

WIDE DRESSES
Elizabeth I
When: 1574 **Where:** England

In passing the Sumptuary Statutes Elizabeth set some curbs on the dress of various strata of society, at court in particular, but she still led the way for major trends. Her red hair and stark makeup became popular, but one particular trend was the ever-widening skirts on her dresses, made possible by hip bolsters.

NO CORSET
Marie Antoinette

When: 1783 **Where:** France

It says something about the relationship that Marie Antoinette had with the people of France that in moments of both extravagance and humility she managed to outrage the populace. The Austrian princess was well known for her lavish fashions and expensive tastes, much of which was likely exaggerated by a growing republican movement to turn the people against the monarchy. However, it was a painting of Marie wearing a simple cotton dress that caused a sensation. Forgoing a corset that was common at the time, many took the image to be of her in her underwear, leading to it being called a chemise a la reine. In using cotton rather than silk, she was also accused of damaging the French fabric industry. It was scandalous at the time, but would usher in a new trend not long after her death as the Georgian and Victorian eras saw the rise of chemise dresses.

DOUBLE-BREASTED SUIT
Charles, Prince of Wales

When: 1980s **Where:** UK

Perhaps enjoying some of the limelight that marriage to Diana gave him, Prince Charles' fashion choices were often influential in their own right. A notable example is his preference for double-breasted blazers, which massively increased in popularity at the height of his and Diana's popularity together.

KELLY BAG
Grace Kelly

When: 1956
Where: Monaco

While Princess Grace of Monaco, aka Grace Kelly, should take most of the credit for the popularity of the 'Kelly Bag', some credit ought to be handed to Alfred Hitchcock and the costume designer Edith Head as well. The celebrated film director gave approval for Head to purchase accessories from Hermés of Paris for the film *To Catch A Thief*, and one of the items she bought was a Haut à Courroies bag costing over £3,000. Kelly not only loved the bag on set, she started using it all the time. She made the bag famous when she used it to screen herself against photographers after her marriage to Rainier III, Prince of Monaco. The bag's popularity exploded to such an extent that Hermés renamed it the Kelly Bag in her honour.

RED HIGH HEELS
Louis XIV

When: 1660s
Where: France

When Louis XIV ascended the throne in 1643 it was not uncommon for men to wear shoes with very large heels. Charles II, for instance, was known to wear them, making his 1.85-metre stature all the more impressive. For Louis, however, the heel was a little more important to him. Standing 1.63-metres tall, he was sensitive about his height and wanted to appear more imposing by wearing a 10cm heel. To accentuate the point, he would have the heel and sole dyed red, which was an expensive colour to use in the 1660s. A king's fashions tend to cause a trend, but Louis made red heels even more exclusive when he passed an edict limiting their use to members of the court. Now, the red heel for men was not only fashionable but also a great status symbol.

20 royal fashion trends

EMPRESS STYLE
Catherine The Great

When: 1762 **Where:** Russia

As the soon-to-be Catherine the Great prepared to instigate the overthrow of her husband Peter III, she put on the uniform of Captain Alexander Talyzin, a member of the Life Guards Semionovsky Regiment. This was the old uniform that had existed since Peter the Great and had been replaced by Peter III for something more Prussian in style. It was a signal to the military that she was with them in their distaste for Peter's Prussian leanings, despite being from Prussia herself. The coup was a success, she became empress of Russia, and from then on would incorporate elements of traditional Russian dress and uniform dresses into her wardrobe to reaffirm her dedication to her adopted land.

LEISURE WEAR
Edward VIII

When: 1920s **Where:** UK

Few royal men have had as much of an impact on national fashions as the then-Prince of Wales did during the 1920s. From early on he advocated for what he called "dress soft" clothing, putting comfort ahead of the more formal attire usually favoured by members of the royal family. What this meant in reality was that he adopted the era's move towards leisure wear, or sports casual, such as heavily patterned sports coats. The prince's enthusiasm for these more informal fashions had a massive impact on the nation. While the prince himself was not always well liked by the people (less so after his abdication from the throne in 1936), his sense of style was always closely followed and imitated by those who could access the same Savile Row tailors as he could. Edward essentially established the place of 'smart casual' in every man's wardrobe from then on.

FRENCH HOOD
Anne Boleyn

When: 1520s
Where: England

Prior to Anne Boleyn's arrival in Henry VIII's court, the fashion for women had been to wear a gable hood (early portraits even depict her wearing one). But as her influence grew she brought the French Hood into vogue, with its rounder, softer design. Interestingly, upon her death the gable began to be used again.

UNBUTTONED WAISTCOAT
Edward VII

When: 1901 **Where:** UK

While sometimes challenged as an apocryphal story, fashion historians seem to agree that the custom of leaving the bottom button of a waistcoat undone, which exists to this day, was started by Edward VII. Fond of a waistcoat, his increasing waistline is supposed to have influenced his choice, which quickly caught on as a trend.

THREE-PIECE SUIT
Charles II

When: 1666 **Where:** England

Abandoning French fashion, Charles II declared that his court would be adopting what was known as the Persian vest, a long waistcoat, from around 1666 onwards. This essentially began the trend of a coat or jacket over a waistcoat with some form of leg covering, which we would today consider a three-piece suit.

Charles IX of Valois in some fashionably puffy hose

The ill-fated Charles I was no stranger to larger-than-life fashion

For the love of
CODPIECES

When skirts, tights, and frills were the hallmarks of masculinity

―――

Written by Mark Dolan

Walking through the womenswear section of a clothing shop into the mens' section is to feel the clouds darken the atmosphere as different shapes, colours and styles give way to plain blue, black and grey jackets, trousers and waistcoats. It wasn't always like this. In the 400-odd years before the French Revolution, men (well, rich ones) would be adorned in bright colours, luxurious fabrics, and extravagant silhouettes.

'Fashion' in a way we might recognise first emerged in the second half of the 14th century, when men started to don garments more shapely and tailored than the simple, if practical, tunic. The gipon, or doublet, was the first iteration of this, a garment that was cinched around the waist and padded around the chest. Coming only to the knees, it was almost immediately dubbed indecent by the moralists of the day.

In the early 15th century, wealthy men would wear their doublets, now often made of silk rather than wool, under a long outer garment called a houppelande. Men and women alike wore houppelandes, but it was upper-class men whose clothes would be the most colourful, expensive and extravagant. While almost everyone in the French court - the hub of fashion at this time - was wearing a houppelande, there were ways to make them stand out. They could be brightly coloured, either full length or 'bastard length' (with the hem around the mid-calf), with cavernous funnel-shaped bombard sleeves or baggy poke sleeves that narrowed at the wrist, and would be elaborated by the technique of dagging (cutting shapes out of the edges of sleeves and hems). Fashionable full-length houppelandes would sometimes be so long as to pool around the wearer's feet, while bombard sleeves quickly grew so oversized that in Italy a law was passed limiting them to a maximum width of four feet. Finishing off a look with a pair of poulaines - extremely pointy shoes - meant that the fashionable early 15th-century man would be almost unable to move. Luckily, if you were able to put together such an outfit, there wasn't a huge amount of moving that needed to be done.

In mid-15th century Northern Europe, partly thanks to the influence of Duke Philip the Good of Burgundy, who wore exclusively black clothes, menswear shifted away from bright colours and long, flowing outerwear towards tighter fitting shorter outer garments and darker colours. The preferred look of the duke and his followers consisted of a tight-fitting doublet - with the ties pulled apart to reveal a sliver of the linen undershirt - hose, which were fitted leggings tied

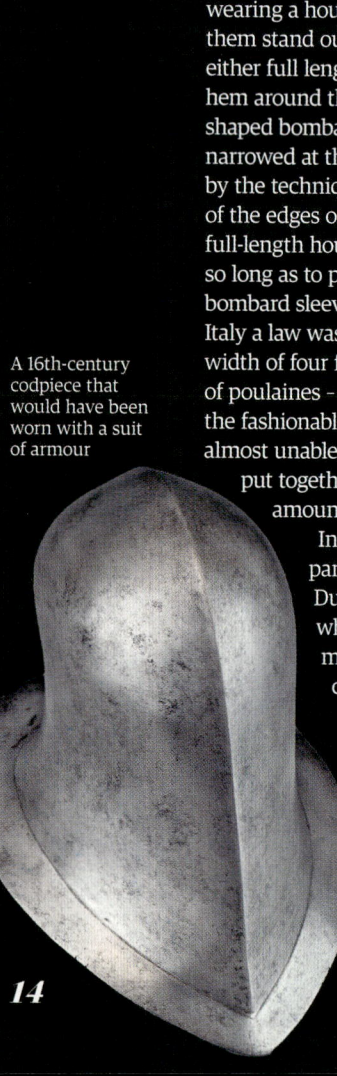

A 16th-century codpiece that would have been worn with a suit of armour

For the love of codpieces

Henri I of Lorraine's unwieldy starched ruff

Henry VIII with his broad-shouldered gown and prominent codpiece

to the doublet with laces, and a luxurious fur-lined houppelande, perhaps lined with gold thread.

The doublet and hose, the contemporary staples of menswear, didn't meet or overlap in the middle. Attached together by laces, if a man wasn't wearing another layer over the top, his underwear (a decidedly unsexy pair of plain linen drawers) would be visible. As the outer layers of clothing got shorter and shorter in the mid-late 15th century, there was a need to change the hose from two separate pieces for each leg into a complete lower garment. Enter the codpiece. Initially a purely functional part of this new garment, it would soon take on a fashionable life of its own.

One man who took lavishness to a new level was Philip the Good's son, Charles the Bold. Although, at first glance, Charles' gaudy jewel-encrusted attire seems a far cry from his father's all-black wardrobe, there is some continuity between them. Where Philip had heavy jewellery and gold thread, Charles used various precious stones, and both were fond of luxurious Italian fabrics. In January 1474, appearing to formally take possession of the Duchy of Burgundy, Charles turned up wearing a suit of armour that had jewels embedded into the arm and knee plates, with a giornea, an Italian-style coat with cut-out sleeves, to allow his jewel-encrusted arms to show through, that was itself embroidered with huge pearls.

Some of Charles' most notable pieces are his multiple jewel-covered ducal hats. In 1471, he commissioned a hat made of steel, covered with gold and with layers of rubies and pearls running around it. Another one appeared in 1475 made of black velvet, covered with rubies, pearls and diamonds, packed so close together that the gold plume that topped it was barely visible.

A TALE OF TWO BEARDS

How the French king's chin changed English court fashion

One of the most fashionable men of the 16th century was the French king François I, a monarch who certainly had a good eye, purchasing the *Mona Lisa* directly from Leonardo da Vinci in 1518. After becoming king in 1515, he quickly became known for his love of fashion, particularly the fabrics and styles of Italy.

François' fashion choices heavily influenced contemporary high French fashion, but his impact was also seen in a concentrated way across the Channel, where the young Henry VIII closely followed his lead, as a (somewhat friendly) rivalry grew between the two. Notably, after hearing that François had grown out his beard, Henry stopped shaving himself, and beards were thrust back into fashion in both the French and English courts. The famous meeting of the two – The Field of the Cloth of Gold – at Balinghem in France in 1520 saw the two try to outdo each other in their display of power and wealth, which, of course, incorporated their clothing and jewellery, including the eponymous cloth of gold, a fabric with thin threads of gold woven through to make them shimmer.

François I was perhaps the first bearded fashionista

15

Louis XIV in full court dress, featuring the red heels and big wig he was known for

LOUISBOUTINS
400 years before Christian Louboutin, red heels made their debut in France

Louis XIV, the Sun King, was another French monarch who loved and influenced fashion. While one of his transformational innovations was the justaucorps, the long overcoat that would end the 350-year reign of the doublet, two of his others concern the head and the feet. The first was his adoption of a long, flowing curly periwig. His particular wig was full at the bottom and rose to two horn-like points at the top of his head. Before long, periwigs were dominant among the upper class of French society, as well as in England. Towards the end of the century, an aging Louis began to powder his wigs white to match his age, and almost immediately across France and England men would begin powdering their wigs to follow, regardless of whether their age suited it. A large powdered wig, if made from human hair, could cost the equivalent of over £2,000.

In addition, Louis' shoes made a range of statements. Following the style that had preceded, his high-heeled shoes (Louis was just 5'4" tall) were covered in silk, brocade or other expensive materials, ornately decorated, and adorned with rosettes or buckles, sometimes made of cut glass. His unique addition was to have a bright red heel. His heels would be covered in red morocco leather or painted red, a style which became a hallmark and subsequently a trend throughout the French court. Louis' decorative heels didn't stop there, though. In addition to the red, he also wore heels painted with landscapes, battle scenes and, it is thought, even risqué portraits.

At the end of the 15th century, young men began to forego any outer garment at all, while the doublet and hose, which were still the predominant men's garments, got tighter and tighter. Hose were skin-tight, while doublets became intentionally too small, leading to gaping down the centre of the chest and a gap between doublet and hose at the back, occasionally covered by a small skirt. To add to the bold look, many men wore parti-coloured clothes, with contrasting colours for the constituent parts of their garments. The ideal look for the fashion-conscious man at this time was to give an impression of being colourfully nude.

By the 16th century, parti-colouring and pointy poulaines fell out of favour for layered colours and broad-toed duckbill shoes, while the new fashion of slashing or pinking emerged. Slashing and pinking involved cutting small slits into outer garments to show the colour of the layer beneath; an effect also achieved by paning - a style of constructing sleeves or hose using parallel strips of fabric joined only at the ends. Brightly coloured skin-tight hose, complete with codpiece, held up with garters and slashed to reveal a contrasting under layer, were the height of fashion for noble young men throughout the continent.

Although in some parts of Europe, notably Spain, dark, demure clothing gained popularity, in other areas, particularly Germany, menswear was anything but. A great example of early 16th-century German fashion is Lucas Cranach the Elder's portrait of Duke Henry the Pious,

A reconstruction of one of Charles the Bold's bejewelled golden hats

> *"Tailors eventually became quite playful with what a codpiece could be"*

whose red doublet and hose and black gown are pinked to within an inch of their lives to show the bright yellow fabric worn underneath, with the understated look finished off with heavy gold chains and green garters.

The 1520s saw accessories become a standout feature, with upper-class men frequently carrying a sword and a pair of gloves (generally of fine material such as kidskin), while proto-ruffs - upturned collars with decorative frills - also started to appear. Into the next decade, fashion at court in England and Northern Europe was led by Henry VIII. The hallmarks of Henry's overtly masculine image were the extremely broad shoulders of his gown, and his prominent codpiece. Although the overall shape is familiar to modern ideas of masculinity, the embroidered fabrics, frills and tassels that were popular in this era are far removed from the sleek, sharp lines of modern menswear.

It was in this period, around the mid-16th century, that the codpiece really had its heyday. It became a key part of the male image, often padded, coloured or shaped to be particularly prominent, in some cases poking through a tailor-made gap in a doublet. Tailors eventually became quite playful with what a codpiece could be, with some even used as pincushions!

In the second half of the century, although codpieces continued to be popular, the silhouette narrowed dramatically. The broad-shouldered look of Henry VIII was replaced by a more natural, slim shape. As the upper body slimmed, the lower body bloomed, with hose getting shorter and wider. The new style was for bombasted hose, which were padded around the upper thigh, and often paned, eventually blooming to the enormous melon hose. Around the same time, codpieces started to shrink and collars began to grow, with the frilled ruff gaining traction, spread initially by Robert Dudley, Elizabeth I's favourite, and getting bigger until it reached 'platter-size' in the 1580s.

While the slimmer silhouette remained the preference for late-16th-century men, a new trend emerged for a protruding lower part of the doublet, known as a peascod. The garment would be made with this rounded aspect, exclusively bulging at the front over the top of the hose, while the rest of a man's waist would remain slim, making it obvious

For the love of codpieces

Duke Philip the Good of Burgundy in his trademark all-black

A young King Charles I in roomy petticoat breeches

that the impression of the overhanging belly was out of stylistic choice rather than necessity.

The early 17th century saw the peascod sucked back in to revert to the fully slim upper body, while hose stayed very full but extended down the leg, into breeches that would go down below the knee, with stockings below. While there wasn't a major overhaul of the men's clothing at court, there was a new style; decorative melancholia, with men opting for open shirts, unbuttoned doublets, creased or ruffled fabrics and an overall impression of dishevelment. This fashionable countenance didn't dominate though, and many men were still dressing sharply, often sporting the new pointed doublet that swept France and England in the 1630s, sometimes newly paired with knee-high leather boots and the 'leg-of-mutton' breeches that had replaced short puffy hose.

These long leather boots quickly took off, and were embellished often with decorative down-turned flaps at the top, trimmed with lace, and featuring butterfly-shaped latchets for fastening. The high, starched ruffs of the late 16th century also faded away, with falling lace collars the vogue of the early 1600s.

During much of the early-mid 17th century, war – first the Thirty Years' and then the English Civil War – halted the progress and lavishness of fashion, but a few notable changes took place, not least the early development of what would become the cravat. As long cascading hair become stylish, the wide lace collars of the late 16th and early 17th centuries became obscured, and some noblemen took to tying them in a bow at the front so they would remain visible and prominent. In England, under Cromwell's rule, clothing became generally more subdued, though there was a burgeoning fashion, here and throughout Europe, for excessive use of ribbon for decorating edges, with ruffles also emerging from the cuffs and hem of doublets.

By the 1660s, breeches had billowed out more, but without being gathered at the hem. Instead, they hung straight but extremely wide, gaining the name of 'petticoat breeches' and being wide enough for someone to put both legs through one side, as Samuel Pepys wrote of a Mr Townsend doing, not noticing his mistake all day. Of course, these were copiously adorned with ribbon. One surviving outfit, comprising a doublet and pair of petticoat breeches belonging to the politician Edmund Verney, used a total of 216 yards of ribbon for decoration!

Around the same time, Louis XIV introduced a new type of outer garment to the French court: the justaucorps. This was a long, largely shapeless overcoat with short sleeves, drawn from military uniform. Charles II soon introduced a similar garment, a collarless long overcoat, to the English court, where it led to the simplification of petticoat breeches, and the widespread adoption of the cravat. The frilly nature of the new necktie aligned perfectly with the taste for ribbon and ruffles.

The dominance of the justaucorps, which left only the front of the doublet visible, led to them being simplified, with only the front made of embroidered or decorative material. Similarly, breeches once again shrank closer to the leg as visibility was reduced.

In the 18th century, men's outfits retained some stability, with a basic outfit consisting of breeches, a waistcoat and a long overcoat, often with a cravat. Although excessive ribbons and ruffles had fallen out of favour, the garments would be made from fine materials, silks and brocades, and elaborately embroidered. While the basic silhouette remained relatively consistent, wealth was displayed through materials, down to the buttons and thread used to construct the garments.

In an echo of the earlier taste for fashionable dishevelment, in the early 18th century, some wealthy men, particularly those of an artistic or literary bent, such as Jonathan Swift, would sit for their portraits in their informal morning or nightgowns; loose, flowing garments that conveyed a kind of elegant undress.

Towards the middle of the century, the bottom of men's coats began to flare out again, and the sleeve cuffs broadened, but otherwise, there was relatively little change in garments. During this period, in England, while expensive materials and stylish embellishment were still used, the most spectacular outfits were found on the continent. As the century drew towards its close, frock coats grew more form-fitting, and although stylish and lavishly made, were relatively simple in construction and silhouette. As the English style gained popularity among the French, waistcoats were made more decorative, with designs often inspired by nature, literature or even popular theatre. At the end of the 18th century, though, the upheaval of the French Revolution would change the development of men's fashion indelibly.

17

How to SEW AN ELIZABETHAN RUFF

The ultimate Tudor fashion statement

While some bishops still wear them and Vivienne Westwood dallied with them on the catwalk, the ruff is most famously associated with Elizabeth I. Emerging in the early 16th century, the ruff began life as a simple collar on the edge of a shift but over the decade became more elaborate as multiple layers, blackwork embroidery, decorative edging and lace became the fashion. Because of its natural springiness linen was the fabric of choice, much finer than the linens we can find today, and by the end of the decade elaborate pleating, starching, waxing and wire under-structures had been utilised to create these fripperies of fashion.

Inspiration to make your ruff can be found in portraits of high society of the age, and you can easily chart their prominence and decoration through the Elizabethan era.

Hand stitching
Running stitch and whip stitch are the names of the hand stitches needed to construct a ruff.

Drawing threads
Use a technique called Drawing a Thread to find the grain of your linen when cutting your strips.

Flat fell seams
Join the strips, sew a seam and cut one side back. Fold the other in then over to hide all raw edges and whip stitch in place.

Hand sewn eyelets
Use waxed linen thread and button hole stitch to sew an eyelet. Buttons, hooks and eyes are also seen on extant ruffs.

Frilly bits
Period lace is difficult to find, using a small cotton lace is most accurate and can help to measure the pleats.

Waxing thread
To ensure your thread doesn't tangle as you work, run it through clear beeswax before you start sewing.

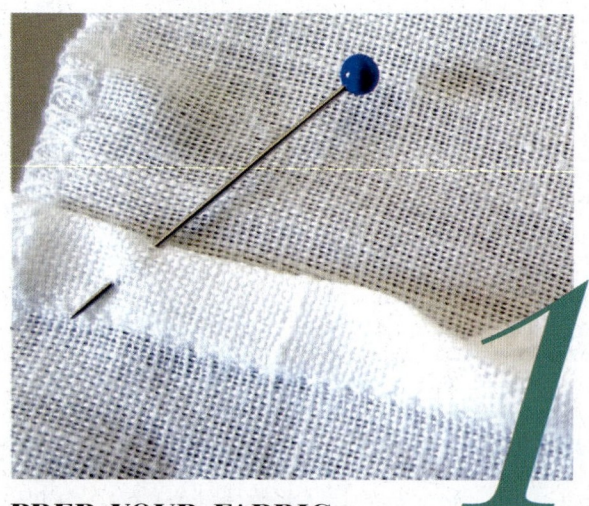

WHAT YOU'LL NEED...

- HALF A METRE OF WHITE LINEN, 1.5M WIDE & 5M WHITE LACE 2CM WIDE OR LESS
- LINEN THREAD AND CLEAR BEESWAX
- BASIC SEWING SUPPLIES (NEEDLES, SCISSORS, RULER)
- STARCH

1. PREP YOUR FABRIC
Cut three strips of linen 7.6cm (3") wide and the width of the linen. Sew together with a flat fell seam to form one strip. Cut another piece of linen 41cm (16") wide and 20cm (8") deep for the neck band. Iron each short edge of the neck band in 1cm (0.5"), then in half lengthways. Fold each long edge in again to the middle and iron again.

2. HEM AND DECORATE
Use an overlock stitch to neaten all edges of your combined linen strip - please note, you're best using a sewing machine for this. Then, using a running stitch, hem the strip up 6cm (0.25") then sew on your lace. Iron the unhemmed edge as straight as possible to give the finished product a crisp look.

How to sew an Elizabethan ruff

HOW NOT TO... MAKE AN ELIZABETHAN RUFF

None of the stitches or techniques needed to make an Elizabethan ruff are very complicated however accurate measuring, marking and cutting is imperative and can often be the most challenging part of ruff making. For instance if you cut your fabric off grain your ruff will 'twist' when it is finished and feel awkward to wear. Cutting fabric along the weft of the fabric your cartridge pleats will be wild and springy.

Whilst this looks terribly romantic and can be used to create a different look, neat pleats it does not make! For this example use a quilting guide to mark the cartridge pleat points. As the breakdown of the inches are marked in a square you can very easily measure both upwards and downwards accurately. If you mark these points incorrectly the pleats will not lie flat and your ruff will look messy very quickly.

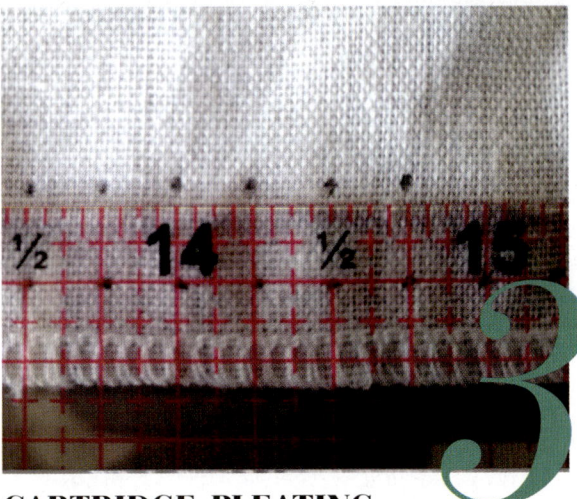

3 FAMOUS RUFF LOVING LADIES

MARY, QUEEN OF SCOTS
SCOTLAND, 1558-1560
Ruffs of the mid 16th century often had decoration along the edge in black, gold or silver.

QUEEN ELIZABETH
ENGLAND, 1573-75
The detachable ruff arrived, and extant examples show efforts by the maker to make a Ruff reversible. Laundry day was made a little easier as ruffs could simply be turned over and worn again!

ANNA DE LOOPER
NETHERLANDS, C. 1627
While closely associated with Elizabethan England, ruffs were worn all over Western Europe during the 16th century.

3 CARTRIDGE PLEATING
Mark a series of small dots 6.35mm (0.25") in and parallel to the unhemmed edge and 6.35mm (0.25") apart. Mark a second line of small dots (0.5") in from the edge, 6.35mm (0.25") apart and directly above the first line. Using a piece of thread approximately 10cm (4") longer than the linen strip, tie a knot in one end and sew in the first line of dots.

4 GATHER YOUR RUFF
Divide your neck band into quarters and mark them with a pin. Repeat for your linen strip. Pull evenly on the gathering threads and gather up the each section of the linen strip to each size of each quarter of the neck band until the strip is the same size as the neck band. Take your time and arrange the pleats as evenly as possible as you work. Tie off.

5 ATTACH THE NECK BAND
Fold out your neck back and with right sides together, whip stitch onto the ruff above the first stitching line of gathering. You do not need to sew through to the other side, just along the top of the pleats. Make your stitches about 6cm (0.25") long. Repeat for the back, then whip stitch the ends closed. Make an eyelet in each end above the ridge of the gathers.

6 ARRANGE YOUR SETTS
Finally, wash the ruff and starch it - you can use a spray starch, but historically they would have made a potato starch (brought back from the New World to Elizabeth's England in 1584). Then arrange the pleats - or 'setts' as they were known - with your fingers so they are even and approximately 4cm (1.5") high. It's ready to wear once dry!

BIGGER *is better*

Charting the evolution of European women's fashion through the Middle Ages and beyond

Written by Emily Staniforth

From the end of the Roman Empire to the French Revolution, European fashion quite literally expanded. Women's outfits transformed from plain and practical designs to extravagant and voluminous garments. Clothing became more exaggerated and skirts ballooned, becoming movement-restricting statements of grandeur and wealth. But was bigger really better? The women of the Middle Ages certainly seemed to have thought so.

In the year 476, the Western Roman Empire crumbled, sending shockwaves through wider Europe. However, European fashion continued to be heavily influenced by the Romans, and very little changed in terms of what people wore on a day-to-day basis. Tunics dominated both male and female fashion, and these were typically worn over the top of a loose-fitting shirt, sometimes referred to as a chemise. For women, tunics were full length and grazed the ground, covering them entirely. For men, however, tunics could either be floor-length or knee-length. During this period, clothing tended to swamp a woman's body, with most clothes being loose fitting and straight, and tightened using simple accessories like belts. Natural fibres such as wool and linen were the choice of material for clothing, and for those who were members of the upper class of society, silk was also popular. Detailing and design varied across regions, but by the 12th century tunics for women began to become more structured, with fabric being gathered at the waist to create a more silhouetted shape.

An example of a robe à la française dress from the late 1700s

Bigger is better

From around 1350, clothing for medieval women became increasingly tailored. At this time, the Italian Renaissance was beginning to take root and would go on to have an enormous cultural impact on the majority of Europe. The foundations of the Renaissance saw emphasis placed on the values and styles of the ancient Greek and Roman worlds, and as a result a renewed interest in the human form began to sweep across Europe along with new Renaissance ideals. Creating more structured clothing allowed women, in particular, to adhere to this new appreciation of the body and move away from the straighter, more loose-fitting clothes of the previous centuries.

As well as becoming more form-fitting, the necklines of dresses began to be made lower to show off a woman's bust. An added piece of clothing also became popular during the 14th century, which was worn over the top of a woman's tunic or dress. The garment was called a surcoat and was similarly popular in men's fashion trends as it was in women's. For men, the surcoat was worn over armour to aid in identifying what side a soldier was in while in the midst of battle. For women, the surcoat simply provided an extra stylish layer, with sleeveless and sleeved versions both worn. The garment was also floor-length and thus gave an extra layer of skirt that added some volume to the shape of a dress.

> "Creating more structured clothing allowed women to adhere to this new appreciation of the body"

During this period, one woman became the trendsetter of the moment. Her name was Isabeau of Bavaria and in 1385 she had become the Queen of France when she married King Charles VI. Her royal standing gave her the two things needed to become a fashion icon: a public platform and a lot of money. Isabeau followed the fashion of the time by wearing dresses with long skirts that were cinched at the waist and worn over the top of a chemise and an undergown to create a shaped silhouette. Her gowns were noted for being beautifully bejewelled with rare gems as well as trimmed with expensive ermine. She wore deep, regal colours like burgundy and gold, and was particularly fond of an elaborate braided hairstyle that was piled on top of her head and covered with a tall cone-shaped double hennin headpiece. These headdresses were so tall that it is alleged that doors had to be enlarged to accommodate them. Despite her excellent fashion

This portrait of Elizabeth I shows an example of the more elaborate, larger skirted dresses worn by wealthy women in the 16th century

RUFFING IT UP

The expansion of the pleated neck collar

In the 16th century, it wasn't just skirts that grew bigger and bigger. The ruff became an essential fashion statement among the European aristocracy and originated from the Elizabethan period, when this pleated collar first became popular. A separate garment that could be added to outfits, the ruff was completely impractical and served no purpose other than as a display of one's wealth and social standing. Worn by men and women alike, the ruff could be worn in the same way by both sexes as a simple collar that expanded outwards from the neck. However, developing with women's fashionable low necklines of the 16th century the ruff was adapted for women into a half collar. These ruffs expanded outwards and upwards behind the neck, but the front was open to allow for a plunging neckline.

Women did, however, also continue to wear full ruffs and even subscribed to the expanding styles that became popular as English starch was produced from the 1560s. This starch helped to stiffen the ruffs, meaning they could be made bigger and wider than they ever had been before. The largest of ruffs was the 17th-century cartwheel ruff which could reach up to eight inches in width and was popular in countries like England, the Netherlands and France. While the size of a ruff indicated wealth, so too did the decoration of a ruff. Some women had their ruffs made from fine linens with intricate lace detailing to display their affluence, while others adorned them with jewels and pearls. The heavier the decoration, the starchier the ruffs had to be made. Eventually, in the second half of the 17th century, fashionable ruffs began to diminish in size until they ceased to be fashionable altogether.

Hortensia del Prado, a Dutch noblewoman, is painted here wearing a sizeable ruff in 1599

A 15th century Burgundian noblewoman wears an elaborate patterned dress

Bigger is better

"What was fashionable started to differ from place to place across Europe"

sense, Isabeau's extravagant spending on expensive clothes did little to help her reputation with those who criticised the indulgences of the French court. Furthermore, while fashion trends had come to be more appreciative of the female form, the low necklines of Isabeau's outfits, and those of her ladies in waiting, drew comment from some who believed the choice to be a little too risqué.

As time progressed and the 15th century came around, it wasn't just women like Isabeau of Bavaria who started to occupy more and more space… literally. Skirts became fuller and longer, while necklines continued to sit lower. What was fashionable started to differ from place to place across Europe, more so than it had done since before the Romans, with many nations having their own variations on wider stylistic trends. But, like in any society, there were still those who were at the forefront of fashion. The influencers of that time were the Burgundians, who occupied a powerful position in Europe as a prosperous state. At the rich Burgundian court, the houppelande gown began to grow in popularity among women who wanted to display their wealth. Similar to the surcoat of earlier centuries, the houppelande was a gown popular with both men and women that was worn over the top of other clothes. Unlike other dress styles of the time, the houppelande was designed with a V-shaped neckline with a high collar. It would have been a heavy garment made from a lot of material, intended to flaunt the wearer's wealth, as a larger amount of material signified they could afford to buy more. As a result, the houppelande gowns of

Isabeau of Bavaria was a renowned medieval trendsetter

The extreme wedding dress worn by a Swedish queen in 1766

the 15th century were made to have large sleeves and huge skirts to conspicuously make use of as much material as possible.

Aside from the Burgundian trendsetters, Beatrice d'Este was one of the most prominent fashion icons of the era. The Duchess of Bari and Milan took her inspiration from elsewhere in Europe, particularly Spain, and was known to ask Milan's foreign ambassadors to keep her abreast of fashion trends across the continent. It is believed that Beatrice even designed some of her own clothes, drawing on Turkish designs she may have seen while in Venice.

The advent of the 16th century saw increased developments in the size of women's dresses. Voluminous skirts were now accentuated by the whalebone bodices that were becoming more popular. By cinching in the waist even more with these rigid undergarments, it became fashionable for the top half of the body to appear tiny while lower garments ballooned out dramatically. Dresses fashioned in this new style are commonly seen in royal portraits of the era and were loved in the English Elizabethan court where they were a favourite look of Queen Elizabeth I. To create wider skirts, Elizabethan dresses were draped over an inner hooped skirt that helped to create

Pictured third from the left is Isabeau of Bavaria. She is surrounded by her ladies in waiting, all of whom are dressed in the extravagant royal fashion of the time

By the mid-18th century necklines had plunged and skirts had exploded in size

Beatrice de'Este is shown wearing a particularly bold striped dress in this painting

Bigger is better

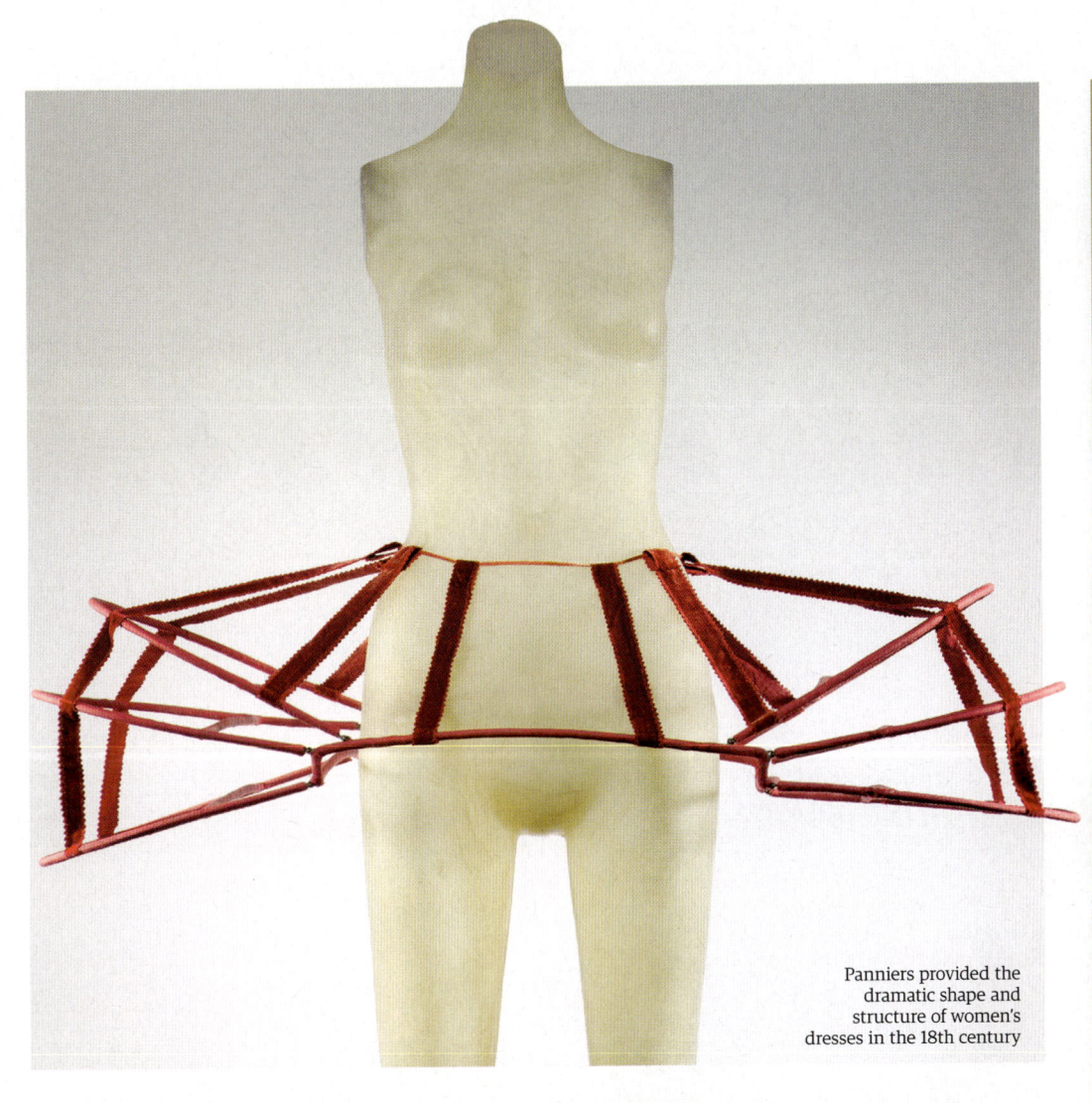

Panniers provided the dramatic shape and structure of women's dresses in the 18th century

"The hoop skirt was brought to England by Catherine of Aragon"

the desired billowing aesthetic. In England, these skirts were called farthingales but in Spain, where these garments were first fashionable a century earlier, they were called verdugado. It is believed that the hoop skirt was brought over to England by the Spanish princess Catherine of Aragon when she arrived in the country to marry the Prince of Wales Arthur Tudor in 1501 (After Arthur's death, Catherine married his younger brother Henry, becoming the first of Henry VIII's six wives).

The farthingale style of dress continued to be a popular choice for women at the forefront of fashion into the 17th century, when skirts only became bigger and better and other aspects of female clothing became more extreme. Necklines were dropped even lower, so much so that they barely covered a woman's breasts, and among the European elite outfits became increasingly bedazzled with fine materials and jewels. The farthingale was added to to create wider silhouettes, with extra material layers tied around a woman's waist to accentuate her behind. By the time the 18th century rolled around, fashionable female attire had arguably reached the peak of extravagance. A number of styles of gown had developed which utilised the silhouette created by hoop skirts of different varieties, like the mantua dress which featured a large train attached to its back or the robe à la française which opened at the front to expose more beautiful material.

France had become the fashion capital of Europe, but this was to be short lived. With the beginning of the French Revolution in 1789 social change was afoot and more attention was being paid to the indulgences of the elite classes in Europe. In response to the atmosphere of rebellion brought about by France's revolutionaries, fashion was dialled down and started to become less extravagant and more modest. Skirts began to shrink, necklines became higher and clothes were designed to be plainer and less decorative and demonstrative. For the wealthy and influential aristocrats who were either caught up in the bloody events of the French Revolution or witnessed it from afar, it was clear that their excessive tastes would no longer be accepted by the masses.

MARIE ANTOINETTE AND THE FRENCH REVOLUTION
The downfall of a fashion icon

If there was one person who could be described as the epitome of 18th-century high French fashion it would have to be Marie Antoinette. Marie married the heir to the French throne in 1770, and became Queen of France in 1774 when her husband was crowned King Louis XVI. Upon her arrival at the French court, Marie eschewed her native Austrian fashions and threw herself into dressing in the finest styles of her new home country, apparently having 300 dresses made every year and abiding by the timeless high-fashion rule of never repeating an outfit. She tended to stick to a pastel colour palette, favouring lilacs and blues over the fashionable deeper colours of earlier centuries. Her gowns were elaborately decorated with ribbons and frills, apparently ignoring the cliché 'less is more'. Many of her dresses were designed in the robe à la française style that was so popular at the French court, and as a result her image made an incredible impact due to the large rounded silhouette created by her clothes. She also indulged in 'pouffe' hairstyles which could reach up to three feet tall and were topped with extravagant feather adornments.

Ultimately, Marie's fashionable style did little to help endear her to the general public, who were becoming increasingly displeased with the extreme spending habits of King Louis. She may have been an icon of the moment (and beyond) but her expensive taste angered the lower class French citizens who could barely afford to feed themselves. In response to the growing resentment, Marie tempered her style and began to dress more simply, but this did not placate her people who saw her attempts as a form of mockery. Eventually, Marie was executed in 1793 after the abolition of the French monarchy.

French queen Marie Antoinette was infamous for her extravagant and over-the-top dress sense

THE ART of embroidery

Unravel the rich history and intricate artistry behind the timeless craft of embroidery

Written by Jessica Leggett

Two women work on their embroidery in this scene painted by 19th-century artist Alexander Hugo Bakker Korff

26

The art of embroidery

Embroidery, the process of decorating fabric and other materials with a needle and thread, is one of the oldest art forms in the world. While the term 'embroidery' is believed to have originated in the 14th century, coming from the French word for embellishment, 'broderie', archaeological evidence suggests that the art form itself dates back thousands of years – though we cannot say where or when needlework originated.

Throughout history, embroidery has been practised by various cultures around the globe, including Egypt, China, and India. It requires a lot of skill and has been used to decorate furnishings, religious objects and clothing. Embroidery on clothing served many purposes, such as decoration and expression, signifying wealth and social status, preserving cultural heritage and oral traditions, and mending or increasing the durability of items. For example, during the Edo period (1603-1868), the Japanese technique of Kogin involved using darning-stitch embroidery to improve the durability of farmers' clothing.

Some of the oldest extant pieces of embroidered clothing were discovered in Egyptian tombs, most notably in the tomb of Tutankhamun (c.1341-1323 BCE). These textiles and garments, including a tunic made for the pharaoh when he was a child, and a floral collar, were decorated with high-quality needlework and stitches familiar to us today, such as the chain stitch, the dot stitch, and the running stitch. These stitches have also been found in surviving examples from ancient China, India and elsewhere, with this evidence demonstrating that embroidery was achieved using natural fibres like linen, wool, and silk.

It is perhaps fair to suggest that the craft of embroidery is predominantly associated with women, with needlework long considered an essential domestic skill for many young women. As an art form, it was typically reserved for women of the nobility, who had the time and the money to afford the materials needed to create decorative embroidered pieces. Yet it is worth remembering that there is little early evidence to shed light on those who embroidered in a non-professional capacity.

We do know that, in the medieval era, both men and women worked as embroiderers in nunneries, monasteries, workshops, and professional guilds to meet the demands for high-quality embroidered items. During this time, embroidered clothing became highly valued as a symbol of wealth, status and power, because of the artisanal skill and expensive materials required to create the intricate designs.

In particular, there was a demand for a style called Opus Anglicanum, Latin for 'English work', a type of English medieval embroidery that produced luxurious and elaborate imagery (taken

A delicately embroidered silk suit, dating from around the late-18th century

RETURN TO LUXURY

How handcrafted embroidery was revived to become a favourite of haute couture design

Clothing production was forever changed during the Industrial Revolution, with the development of new machinery, such as the sewing machine, allowing garments to be quickly and cheaply mass-produced in large factories. However, this also led to the emergence of haute couture, which catered to the desire for custom-made clothing amongst the wealthy.

The father of haute couture, Charles Frederick Worth, designed custom garments for his clients with a focus on craftsmanship, quality, and exclusivity. As a result, many of his designs featured lavish fabrics and intricate hand embroidery that added a personal touch to the clothing. By the 1920s, embroidery had become a staple of luxurious high-end Art Deco eveningwear, with dresses and accessories adorned with beautiful embroidery.

Other designers who utilised exquisite hand embroidery in the decades since include Elsa Schiaparelli, who frequently collaborated with the Parisian embroidery atelier Maison Lesage to bring her avant-garde designs to life, and Christian Dior, who had a passion for botanical designs. In recent years, Chinese couturier Guo Pei has received acclaim for the lavish embroidery she includes in her designs, featuring motifs inspired by Chinese culture such as phoenixes and dragons. Her work was brought to worldwide attention when Rihanna wore Guo's Yellow Empress cape to the 2015 Met Gala, which was decorated with 50,000 hours' worth of hand embroidery.

While embroidery has been in and out of fashion since the 20th century, it has once again seen a resurgence over the last couple of years as designers and consumers look to add individuality to clothing. The fact that embroidery has existed for thousands of years and yet continues to appeal to us today proves just how timeless an art form it is.

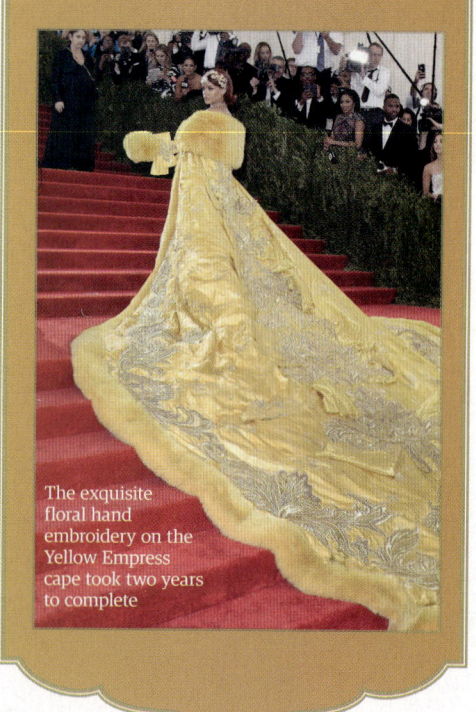

The exquisite floral hand embroidery on the Yellow Empress cape took two years to complete

A sketch depicting zardozi embroiderers working in Delhi, 1870

from the Bible) made with silk, gold and silver thread on linen or velvet with underside couching for the background. Used largely for religious vestments and other liturgical pieces, as well as furnishings, Opus Anglicanum became renowned throughout Europe and sought after by those who could afford such exquisite embroidery - namely royalty, the nobility and churches, with many pieces being traded and given as diplomatic gifts.

Opus Anglicanum is also an example of a luxurious form of embroidery known as goldwork. A type of free-style or surface embroidery - techniques that are not limited by the weave of the fabric and don't require counting threads - goldwork is created with gold or metallic threads and embellishments. Often used for military and ceremonial uniforms historically and today, goldwork is believed to date back at least 2,000 years and likely originated in Asia, where it slowly spread to the West via traders on the Silk Road. According to the V&A museum, goldwork in England reached 'remarkable heights of artistry and technical accomplishment' from 1250 to 1350 with Opus Anglicanum.

Another type of goldwork is zardozi, a traditional technique that originated in Persia and is found in India, Pakistan, Iran, and across Central Asia. This elaborate style of goldwork is worked in gold and silver threads and precious stones, on luxurious materials like brocades, velvets, and silks. Common motifs include floral and geometric designs, animals and birds, and paisley patterns.

Zardozi was notably fashionable between the 17th and 19th centuries when it was used to adorn clothing and accessories, as well as royal tents, wall hangings, and other furnishings. Although there was a decline in zardozi following industrialisation and British rule, it has since seen a revival and is both a popular form of embroidery and a cultural legacy in India and Pakistan today, particularly for bridal wear.

While embroidery was mainly associated with religious clothing and symbolism during the medieval era, it started to be used in more secular contexts by the 16th century. One prevalent embroidery technique that could be found in Spain and Tudor England, especially at the court of King Henry VIII, was blackwork - a type of counted-

The art of embroidery

A panel of British blackwork embroidery, dating from the 16th century

Workers mechanically embroidering fabric with the Schiffli embroidery machine in Nottingham, 1959

Delicate blackwork can be seen here on the cuff of Jane Seymour's dress

thread embroidery which involves counting the number of threads on a piece of fabric to create a uniform pattern.

Blackwork was a monochromatic form of embroidery typically done using black silk thread (although other single colours could be used) on white linen. This technique involved using a Holbein or double-running stitch to create an outline before using chain, stem, or split stitches to create eye-catching geometric, floral and curvilinear designs. It was often used to adorn clothing, including sleeves, collars, cuffs and undergarments, such as smocks, where it would decorate sections that were visible to others when worn. This was to show off the skill of the embroidery that was worn by nobility and royals as a symbol of their wealth and status at court.

By the time of Queen Elizabeth I's reign, blackwork embroidery in England had begun to embrace more naturalistic designs featuring animals, particularly birds, which was likely influenced by the spread of the Renaissance across Europe. During this period, embroidery also started to develop into a popular domestic craft amongst women, with a particular focus on canvas work – also known as needlepoint – embroidery. This form of embroidery involved counting stitches and working them over onto stiff canvases, and it was a suitable choice for decorating upholstery.

Crewel work is another form of embroidery that was stylish in the 16th century and flourished in the 17th century – even though it dates back over 1,000 years and was used to create the famous 11th-century Bayeux Tapestry. This free-style form of embroidery is characterised by the use of two-ply wool yarn, called crewel, on either cotton or linen fabric. It was popular in England and the American colonies, and was used to create vibrant

> "During this period, embroidery started to develop into a popular domestic craft amongst women"

and colourful motifs, including floral and animal designs. These fashionable designs were typically used to decorate household furnishings such as curtains, wall hangings, and furniture coverings. The patterns were influenced by imported fabrics, particularly embroidered ones from China and cotton fabrics from India, the latter of which were brought to 17th-century England through the East India Company.

While many of the techniques discussed so far have used contrast, metallic threads and exotic designs to create embroidery, there is a collection

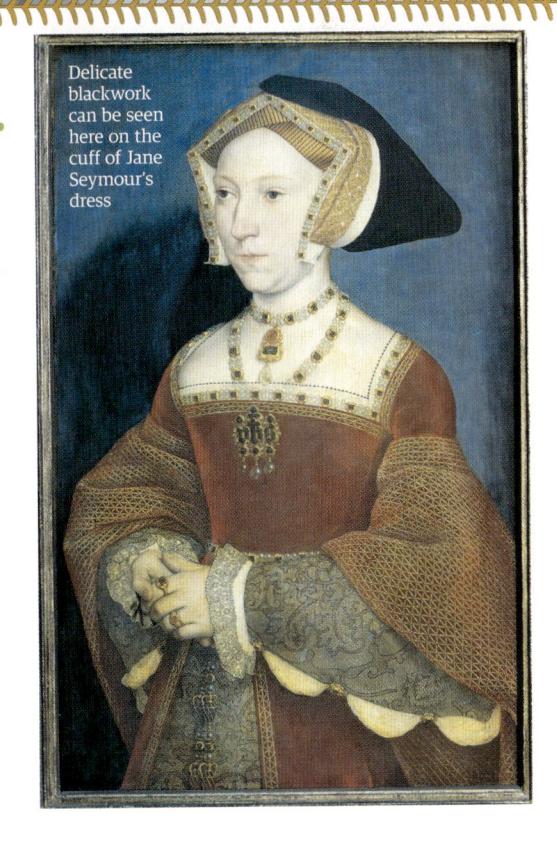

29

of techniques that did the opposite - whitework. Consisting of different counted-thread and freestyle techniques that range from bold and impactful stitches to fine and delicate ones, whitework is the embroidery of white thread onto white material.

Although whitework had been around for centuries, created by highly skilled embroiderers, it gained popularity during the 19th century in Europe and America when it was picked up as a hobby among middle-class women. Seen as a cheaper alternative to lace, it was frequently used to decorate nightclothes, ecclesiastical garments, bed and table linens, baby clothing, christening outfits, dresses, blouses, and more. One type of whitework that is still prevalent today is broderie anglaise, a technique that produces a lace-like embroidery by using a satin stitch and eyelets and can often be found on shop-bought clothing.

It was also during the 19th century that the art of embroidery was significantly influenced by the Industrial Revolution. The invention of the first hand embroidery machine by Josué Heilmann in France in 1828, and later the industrial Schiffli embroidery machine by Isaak Gröbli in Switzerland in 1863, led to the mass production of embroidery from the 1870s onward. As a result, intricately embroidered goods - that had once been labour-intensive and could only be created by hand - became more accessible and affordable to the masses, thereby losing the exclusivity it had held amongst the upper classes.

As demand for handmade embroidered clothing and other items decreased, many professional embroiderers lost their livelihoods. In response to the increase in mass-produced goods, both embroidered and otherwise, the Arts and Crafts

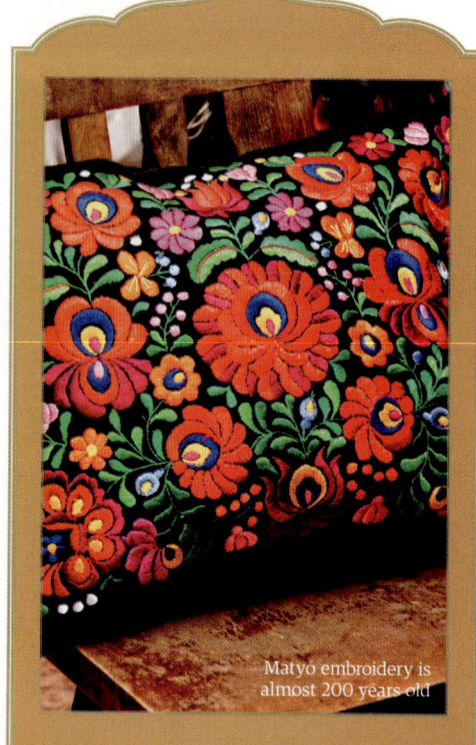

> *"As demand for handmade clothing decreased, many professional embroiderers lost their livelihoods"*

This early-17th-century doublet is an unrivalled example of fashion-forward silk embroidery and pinking (the intentional slits to reveal peeks of the wearer's shirt)

Matyó embroidery is almost 200 years old

PRESERVING HERITAGE

Discover the folk art of Matyó embroidery

Throughout history, embroidery has been used around the world to preserve cultural heritage and identity. An example of this is Matyó embroidery, a traditional Hungarian folk art form originating from the Matyó people, who live primarily in and around the town of Mezőkövesd in northeastern Hungary.

This free-style hand embroidery is known for its floral motifs and vibrant colours including red, blue, green, purple, yellow and black, with these colours meant to symbolise Hungary and Hungarian life. For example, red symbolises joy, yellow symbolises the sun and summer, and green symbolises mourning - the latter was added to the colour palette after WWI. Interestingly, while Matyó embroidery is characterised today by the variety of bright and contrasting colours used, only the colours red and blue were traditionally used until the 1860s.

The embroidery is stitched onto white or black fabric to create embroidered clothing, ceremonial items and even home decor, becoming an irreplaceable part of the community's expression and self-identity. It is also a crucial part of their traditional dress, which is worn by the Matyó during folk dancing and singing.

A traditional folk art that has been passed down from generation to generation, Matyó embroidery was added to UNESCO's Representative List of the Intangible Cultural Heritage of Humanity in 2012. Recognising its importance as a living cultural tradition, UNESCO highlighted that the 'embroidery strengthens interpersonal relationships and community cohesion, while allowing for individual artistic expression'.

The art of embroidery

FAR RIGHT
This chasuble, a liturgical vestment, is decorated with Opus Anglicanum embroidery

RIGHT
A panel decorated with crewel embroidery from 17th-century England

BELOW
The craft of embroidery is often associated with women

movement emerged in Britain and spread across Europe and North America. The movement fought to restore and champion handcrafted goods, craftsmanship, traditional skills, and other values. A key figure in this movement was designer and social reformer William Morris, who advocated for the revival of traditional embroidery techniques. Not only did he teach himself and others embroidery and designed several hand embroideries, but he also supported the Royal School of Needlework, which was founded in 1872.

Few techniques have proved as versatile, global or long-lasting as embroidery. Its popularity across continents and centuries, a multitude of styles, forms and materials, and almost endless applications prove how important it is as an art form. As a technique and practice, it keeps centuries-old traditions and craftsmanship alive, while continuing to find new audiences today as a beloved pastime.

A worker in a sari factory in Rajasthan, India, surrounded by brightly coloured fabrics

LOOKS to dye FOR

Colourful clothes for all is a fairly recent innovation. Before that, colourways were the ultimate in conspicuous consumption – and you could be punished for disobeying the style rules…

Written by April Madden

The newborn princess was clearly destined for greatness. She was the daughter of Byzantine emperor Romanos II and his empress Theophano. The fourth and last of the couple's children, she is remembered by history chiefly because of the imperial family's unique relationship with colour. Although she would go on to marry Vladimir the Great, be crowned Grand Princess of Kiev and become a powerful force in the Christianisation of the Kievan Rus, she is referred to today by her maiden name Anna Porphyrogenita, because of the uniquely colourful circumstances of her birth.

In the ancient and medieval world purple was the colour of greatness, of royalty and of holiness. It's a difficult colour to find naturally, and in the Old World, its only source was a type of sea snail called murex. The ancient Phoenician city of Tyre (now in modern-day Lebanon) was the first to harvest murex and produce the dye, which became known as Tyrian purple. It was difficult, costly and labour-intensive to make. The sea snails could only be found in very particular waters and were not easy to catch. It took vast quantities of them to make even a small amount – around 250,000 snails per tablespoon of refined dye – and the process required time and a lot of manpower. Tyrian purple, then, was incredibly expensive and available in only very limited quantities. It also had a unique property: instead of fading in sunlight, its colour intensified.

Under Tudor England's sumptuary laws only Queen Elizabeth I was allowed to wear cloth-of-gold

For centuries Tyrian purple robes were emblematic of the Byzantine imperial family

"Tyrian purple had a unique property: instead of fading in sunlight, its colour intensified"

This precious and seemingly magical nature made Tyrian purple an obvious choice for the robes of priests in first the old pagan Phoenician religion and later the newer faith of Judaism. Soon, wealthy Persians, Greeks and Romans coveted it too. By the 4th century CE, the only Roman who was allowed to wear Tyrian purple was the emperor himself. This proscription was law across the Roman Empire, of which Byzantium was the Eastern power centre. When Rome fell, Byzantium carried its imperial power - and many of its laws - on into the medieval era. Tyrian purple was restricted to the Byzantine royal house and was only used for dying the silks they wore - the then Roman Emperor of the East, Justinian I, had set up an operation to have the secrets of silk production, and some silkworm eggs, smuggled to Byzantium from China by Nestorian monks in the 6th century CE. By the time Anna Porphyrogenita was born in 963 CE, the Emperor's Palace had a special purple chamber, its walls made from the red-purple gem porphyry and its furniture swagged in Tyrian purple cloth, in which the children of the emperors were born. It gave rise to the phrase 'born to the purple' to denote a royal child who was destined to rule, and to the uniquely medieval concept of porphyrogeniture, in which royal sons who were born after their father acceded his throne outranked the older brothers born before their father was crowned, and were thus more likely to be king. In the 12th century, Henry I of England, fourth son of William the Conqueror, used the idea of porphyrogeniture to justify his claim to the English throne against his older brother Robert Curthose, who became Duke of Normandy instead.

Rules that govern what people can wear are called sumptuary laws, and for centuries they were used to enforce social hierarchies. Sumptuary laws actually govern a wide range of conspicuous consumption - in Ming-dynasty China they were used to regulate how decorative gravestones could be, while in the cities of ancient Greece they were used to try and curb public drunkenness. While many societies claimed that their sumptuary laws were designed to prevent corruption in public offices - in Rome they controlled whose parties magistrates were allowed to go to - in practice they were most often used to limit the luxuries that were available to the wealthy but non-noble classes, and thus became most associated with the most visible outward sign of affluence: clothing. And while they would also cover fabrics, notably silk and velvet, the most obvious feature of clothing that was legislated was its colour. Purple is the most famous example, but there have been others. In China, imperial yellow was reserved for the highest ranking court officials and the emperor's bodyguards. In Elizabethan England, cloth-of-gold was forbidden to all except the queen; in 8th-century Baghdad, Christians had to wear blue to identify themselves.

Colour had been used to denote rank in priesthoods across the globe for centuries. When

Looks to dye for

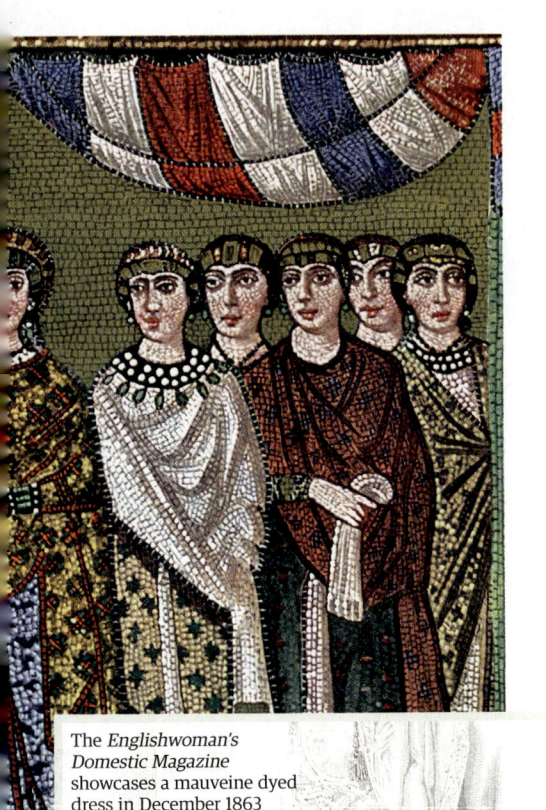

trying to recreate the structures of the ancient druidic faith in the 1970s, modern-day acolytes went back to classical sources, mining texts from the Roman conquest of Britain and cross-referencing them with the dyes available in the British Isles at the time to try and discover what their spiritual ancestors might have worn at different phases of their religious journey. Ancient Celtic legends speak of bards – poet-priests who travelled the land sharing sacred songs and stories – being allowed to wear more colourful cloaks than kings. In the Roman Catholic Church, priests celebrating mass wear different coloured vestments depending on the time of year or whether it's a holy day. Purple, notably, is used at Easter and on the most solemn of occasions.

The earliest dyes all came from natural sources. Yellows and muted reds came from earth pigments like ochre. Blues came from plants such as indigo and woad, or in Morocco from a unique regional variant of murex. Khakis, browns and yellowy greens could be made from lichens, tree bark, moss and leaves. Black came from walnuts; white from lye produced from wood ash. Reds and pinks came from rose madder, henna or a Mediterranean beetle called kermes. Dyestuffs were traded throughout the Old World, their prices reflecting local availability, production costs, quality and ease of use. While some dyes produced strong and colourfast results on their own, many others required the use of a mordant – a substance that helps the dye to set, either by pre-treatment of the fibre, or after dyeing. Alum salts and metals were traditionally used, but they affected the structure and consequently the lifespan of the cloth. The blue and brown of indigo and lichen were common clothing colours as they didn't require a mordant, thus being both cheaper to make and lasting

The Englishwoman's Domestic Magazine showcases a mauveine dyed dress in December 1863

By the early 1900s synthetic dyes were available for home use to give clothes a fashionable new lease of life

VISITOR: "HOW LOVELY! WHY MAUD, HOW DID YOU MANAGE IT ALL?"
MAUD: "EASILY ENOUGH, THESE BLOUSES, UNDERSKIRT, RIBBONS, CUSHION COVERS, IN FACT, EVERYTHING IN THIS ROOM IS DYED WITH THAT WONDERFUL PREPARATION MAYPOLE SOAP."

DISGUSTING DYES
Five dire dyestuffs from history

While many pigments were made from plant sources, other clothing treatments were manufactured from ingredients that might give you the ick. Here are some of them.

1 BABY WASPS
Gall wasps lay their eggs in oak leaf buds which then mutate into galls, or oak apples, weird bulbous growths that protect the growing wasp larvae. Mixed with iron they make a shadowy, purple-toned dark charcoal that was used as dye and writing ink for centuries.

2 OCTOPUS INK
Cephalopods are famous for squirting a cloud of ink to confuse would-be predators, and this could be harvested to make writing ink or dye. Octopus ink is black, squid-ink darkest blue, while brown-inking cuttlefish have given their Latin name to a colour that is associated today with all things retro and vintage: sepia.

3 SEA SNAILS
The unfortunate murex is the source of Tyrian purple. Another variety of the sea snail that is found solely on the coasts of Spain, Portugal and North Africa produces a vivid blue that was known to the ancient Egyptians as tekhelet.

4 BEETLE JUICE
Before the discovery of the Americas, a Mediterranean beetle called kermes or an Asian one called kerria lacca were the sources of crimson dye. Afterwards, the easily harvested cactus-dwelling cochineal bug replaced them. Squashed to extract its red pigment, cochineal or carmine is also used in lipstick and food… yum.

5 TANNING LOTION
Bating is a part of the leather tanning process that prepares animal skins for the process of becoming supple, dyed leather. It consists of softening and removing any leftover hair, fat and connective tissue from the skin using solutions made from urine, faeces, and even minced animal brains. Lovely.

After washing, clothes would be hung on bushes or trees or laid out on rocks to dry and bleach in the sun

WEE WASHES WHITER

Whizz, and the dirt is gone

The advent of laundry detergent and the washing machine were just as important to the commercialisation of colourful clothes as the invention of mauveine. Before that, Victorian women - and it was usually women, even in commercial laundries - had to wash clothes by hand, a long and labour-intensive process involving scalding hot water, scrubbing against a serrated washboard, and wringing water out with a mangle. At least they had soap, even if it was harsh on the skin. Before the 19th century, textiles were most often washed with human urine. In ancient Rome, fullers were the ancestors of the modern laundry service and dry cleaner. They collected urine from the city's public lavatories and used it to wash their clients' togas, pallas, tunics and stolas. In medieval Europe the same substance was referred to as chamber-lye (having been collected from chamber pots). There are very good reasons why urine was used: not only was it easily available, and in quantity, but its ammonia content helped to loosen grease, dirt and stains and to bleach fabrics, notably linens, used for sheets and intimate clothing, which could easily be stained by sweat and other bodily fluids. This bleaching effect meant, however, that dyed clothes were likely to fade, especially when dried in the sun afterwards, so expensive colourful clothes were washed in water alone, with verjuice - a sour, acidic (and expensive) cooking ingredient made from crab-apples or grapes, which was available in white or red varieties and could restore the tone and brightness of colourful dyes - or not at all.

Today there is renewed interest in traditional plant-based pigments as a reaction to fast fashion

Looks to dye for

A woman uses the batik dyeing technique on a piece of fabric in Indonesia

Traditional indigo dye was cheaply easily available throughout Asia so was often used for everyday clothes

> "New natural sources for some pigments were found in the New World"

longer. More vibrant colours that needed setting condemned the garments they were used on to shorter lives and fewer washes. For the poorest, meanwhile, even free and easily accessible natural dye was an unnecessary waste of time. Unbleached homespun cloth, in various shades of off-white or grubby grey, was their unofficial uniform.

For those lucky enough to be able to wear colour, this could be dyed into the thread itself, which was then woven into either a plain single colour or a pattern, like the Celtic bard's multicoloured check. Or a finished item of clothing could be garment-dyed, which although it risked uneven coverage in some nooks and crannies, could also be lavishly decorated using resist techniques like batik or tie-dye (in which pigments are prevented from touching certain parts of the cloth using wax or cord), or block-printed to create complex patterns like Indian paisley or Japanese wagara. For the very wealthiest, cloth could be woven into tabbies, damasks and brocades, which use complex weaving techniques to integrate textures and colours into abstract or formal designs that can appear to shimmer in the light.

With the discovery of the New World, new natural sources for some pigments were found, notably cochineal, which replaced Old World dyestuffs as a cheaper and more easily standardised red, but the production of clothing colours remained largely unchanged from the medieval world right up until 1856. At this point, the discovery of mauveine changed everything.

William Henry Perkins was a young British chemist who was trying to synthesise quinine, a substance found in the bark of a Peruvian tree, which is used to treat and prevent malaria – a disease that the then far-flung British Empire, then in control of vast tracts of the tropical world, was increasingly troubled by. Perkins didn't succeed, but he did accidentally create something else: a chemical dye made from widely available coal tar. Cheap to produce in industrial quantities, mauveine revolutionised Victorian fashion, with London succumbing to a trend that the newspapers called 'The Mauve Measles'. Purple was back on the fashion scene – Perkins even tried to name his dye 'Tyrian Purple' – but this time, it was available to everybody. It was soon followed by synthesised alizarin (red), fuchsine and rosaniline (vibrant rose pinks), a range of sunny yellows, and indanthrone (blue). Unfortunately, however, the new synthetic dyes weren't light-fast – unlike Tyrian purple, they faded in sunlight. It would take until the end of the 19th century and the work of Scottish chemist James Morton to create light-fast chemical dyes. He named them 'sundour' (dour in Scots means 'stubborn against') and had friends who were posted in India test samples of his pigments in the fierce sun there. Morton had to sacrifice the range of chemical colours available in favour of fade-resistance, but his work meant that by the beginning of the 20th century, a rainbow of industrially manufactured, washable, light-resistant colourful clothing was available to all.

'Portrait of Marie Antoinette (1755-1793)' in oil by Dutch-Swedish painter Martin van Meytens and painted around 1767-1768 when Marie was aged 12. Van Meytens gained renown through his portraits of the Austrian court

MARIE ANTOINETTE'S EXTREME *makeover*

Marie Antoinette's marital makeover is enough to give even the most committed bridezilla nightmares

Written by Catherine Curzon

F ew names in history are quite as evocative as Marie Antoinette. Frequently imagined strutting through the palace of Versailles, a galleon perched atop chandelier-skimming hair and with panniers so wide she filled a doorway, she has become one of the most recognisable figures in the history of France. She's also one of the most divisive, a woman who still retains the power to evoke either dreamy sighs or tooth gnashing, thanks to her love of largesse, fashion and the high life.

Yet long before she was queen of France, Marie Antoinette was the considerably less well-groomed Archduchess Maria Antonia of Austria. A teen bride, her wedding preparations were enough to make even the most ardent revolutionary's eyes water.

AN AMBITIOUS MOTHER

Forget dashing princes, swooning princesses and happily ever afters – royal marriage in the 18th century was a serious diplomatic business. With the right match, empires could rise and fall, wars could be ended and the course of history might change forever.

Maria Antonia's shrewd and politically ambitious mother, Maria Theresa, had set her heart on an alliance between the Holy Roman Empire and the French Bourbon dynasty, and what better way than marriage? The obvious candidate among her daughters was young Maria Antonia, and once she had Louis, the dauphin of France, in her sights, nothing was going to stand in her way. With negotiations led by the French court's appointed representative, the Duc de Choiseul, there would be plenty of compromise and piles of cash needed to iron out the various points of contract, but for the young archduchess, the pains were more physical than political. Bringing with her an enormous dowry of 200,000 crowns, the bride-to-be made a tempting financial and dynastic prospect. Considerably less tempting were her looks, manners and wardrobe, and when the family of the groom turned a critical eye on the teenager, they were far from impressed.

Despite her talent for music, Maria Antonia had received only a very limited education. With her unruly hair, girlish manner and rumpled clothes,

Dress to impress

Although no images exist, historians have an idea what Marie's wedding dress might have looked like

CHEMISE
The underwear staple of any lady's wardrobe, a simple chemise was concealed beneath the wedding finery. This would be the only simple thing Marie Antoinette would wear on her big day.

CLOTH OF SILVER MANTUA
The final piece of the puzzle, Marie Antoinette's silver mantua was covered in diamonds and pearls fit for a blushing royal bride.

CLOTH OF SILVER STOMACHER
This V-shaped garment was worn over the stays and beneath the mantua. Ornate and opulent, it matched the rest of the dauphine's gown.

CLOTH OF SILVER PETTICOAT
Billowing out over the panniers, Marie's petticoat was of finest cloth of silver and beautifully decorated.

PANNIERS
Giving 18th Century ladies their unique wide-hipped look, these basket-like hooped devices could be made of anything from whalebone to wood and were sometimes as wide as 3.5 metres.

WHALEBONE STAYS
Don't breathe out! Marie Antoinette owed her perfect poise to tightly laced, restrictive whalebone stays.

SHOES
Just like today, 18th Century brides loved to show off their finest shoes on the big day. Decorated and buckled, they stepped out in style.

STOCKINGS AND GARTERS
Tied around the knee, Marie Antoinette's stockings would have been pristine white.

Marie Antoinette's extreme makeover

she didn't look the part of a dauphine at all. Carefree and with no idea of manners and court etiquette, there seemed to be a lot of work to do. No longer would the 13-year-old be free to roam outdoors with her friends – the time had come for Archduchess Maria Antonia to grow up. Her transformation was entrusted to the Duchesse de Gramont, Choiseul's sister. When it came to French style, she knew exactly what Maria Antonia needed.

WHALEBONE WOES

First on the agenda was clothes. It was a reasonably gentle start to the transformation and soon the carefree girl was learning to negotiate the world in the highly structured and elaborate gowns that were the height of French fashion. Dazzled by patterns, swatches, haberdashers and the finest dressmakers Paris had to offer, Maria Antonia's Austrian home became an outpost of the French dressmaking world. Chief among the challenges faced by the couturiers was convincing the young girl to be laced into whalebone stays. Stiff and restrictive, these uncomfortable undies were central to the foundation garments of her new look. She resisted, but eventually had no choice but to give in and, at the cost of comfort, achieved that perfect dauphine posture.

At this early stage in what would be a long and painful journey from playful girl to poised bride, the excitement and apprehension must have been overwhelming. However, even whalebone stays paled in comparison to the trial that awaited. After all, she could always look forward to escaping the stays at the end of a long day and drawing in a much-needed breath. When it came to more invasive procedures though, things could get a little more permanent, not to mention painful.

THE DENTIST AND THE BANDEAU

If changing Maria Antonia's wardrobe had been an inconvenience, then changing her looks would be nothing short of agonising. When the archduchess smiled, the representatives of the Bourbon court gave a collective intake of horrified breath at the sight of her crooked, far-from-perfect teeth. Still, the families were not about to let such a trifling matter stand in the way of the marriage. In 1768, society dentist Pierre Laveran was summoned to Vienna. He was saddled with the unenviable task of giving the archduchess a mouth fit for a French queen, and he knew just what was required: a few months in the grip of Fauchard's Bandeau.

Taking its name from its inventor – Pierre Fauchard, a pioneer in dental treatment – Fauchard's Bandeau was a very early form of brace made of precious metal. Shaped like a shallow horseshoe, it fit into the mouth of the unfortunate patient and was intended to reshape the dental arch. Along the device were perforations through which gold strands were threaded, and would be tied tightly onto the teeth to secure its position. So tightly fastened to the teeth was the device that, over time, the dental arch would be forced to reshape itself to fit the horseshoe shape of the metal frame. The result was straight teeth and the perfect royal smile.

Months of agonising procedures followed as the dental brace went about its work. Just as she had surrendered to the whalebone stays, the young archduchess had no choice but to endure the pain of this unflattering, invasive dental device with fortitude. Finally and much to the bride's relief, the French court declared themselves satisfied and the agonising bandeau was removed.

Now the bride certainly had a smile fit for Versailles, not to mention rooms stuffed with gowns, hats, shoes and jewels more suited for a poised dauphine than a teenage girl. Under the hawkish eye of the Duchesse de Gramont the physical transformation of Maria Antonia into

These shoes, belonging to Marie Antoinette, are typical of the tastes of the time

> "The Bourbon court gave a collective intake of horrified breath at the sight of her crooked, far-from-perfect teeth"

Marie Antoinette was almost complete. All that remained were a few finishing touches here and there to tame her hair and perfect her make up, but there was a rather bigger obstacle on the horizon.

MINDING HER MANNERS

Far from the poised, dignified queen of her portraits, Maria Antonia cared little for the strict and arcane rules of etiquette that were so vital to a successful life in the Bourbon palaces. It wasn't a question of choice though; if she wanted to survive, she had to learn, and fast. In a court where etiquette and intrigue were the most valuable currency in a woman's arsenal, some serious and urgent improvement was required.

Before she became a candidate for the hand of the dauphin, Maria Antonia loved to spend her free time with friends or playing instruments. She had little concern for court politics and the kind of rivalries that raged at Versailles, but her idyllic childhood was over and the time had come to learn etiquette. It must have seemed to Maria Antonia as though she would never be quite right for her new husband and the laborious and demanding process of becoming a Bourbon surely took its toll as the months went on.

Even the tiniest part of life in Paris was dictated by etiquette and the smallest mistake could result in immense social embarrassment. Eager to please the court, her husband-to-be and her fearsome mother, Maria Antonia did all she could to learn the intricate and confusing rules. It proved a long and difficult process, and even when she was dauphine, she continued to make mistakes. Once installed as queen, Marie Antoinette began to fight back against the politics and rules she hated but for now, that day was a long way off.

Etiquette was one element of her new life that the outgoing young lady would always struggle with. Even after her wedding, she was subjected

41

The fifth and final incarnation of the Royal Chapel at the Palace of Versailles was host to all the major ceremonies of the French monarchy from 1710 onward, including the wedding of Louis XV's son the Dauphin Louis with the Infanta Marie-Thérèse d'Espagne of Spain on 23 February 1745, and the wedding of another Dauphin Louis to Marie Antoinette in 1770

Marie Antoinette had an unfashionably large forehead, but her hairdresser styled her hair to draw attention to her long neck, instead

to intense schooling under the watchful eye of Anne d'Arpajon, Comtesse de Noailles. The hugely experienced Anne had previously served queen Marie Leszczynska and was considered an expert without rival in courtly behaviour, so she was the perfect lady-in-waiting for the new bride. Marie Antoinette would come to despise her and even nicknamed her Madame Etiquette, seeing her as a figurehead for the unyielding propriety she abhorred.

A NEW COIFFURE

So, with teeth and clothes just so and manners a work in progress, it was time to put the finishing touches into place. Sieur Larsenneur, the celebrated hairdresser who had created Madame de Pompadour's famous look, was summoned by to tame and tease Maria Antonia's unruly strawberry blonde curls. He was determined to disguise her unfashionable high forehead while drawing attention to her slender neck, which was considered one of her finest features. When Larsenneur finally put down his comb and

42

Marie Antoinette's extreme makeover

> "He was determined to disguise her unfashionable high forehead while drawing attention to her slender neck"

Archduchess Maria Antonia of Austria, the later Queen Marie Antoinette of France, at the age of 16 years in pastel on parchment by Joseph Krantzinger

unveiled the archduchess, she was the very height of Parisian fashion. Now she looked the part, walked the part and even smiled the part: the wedding of the century could proceed.

On 19 April 1770, Maria Antonia and her brother, Ferdinand, arrived at the Augustinian Church in Vienna. Here she was married to Louis by proxy and the girl who entered the church as Archduchess Maria Antonia of Austria left as Marie Antoinette, Dauphine of France. Just two days after the wedding, Marie Antoinette and an enormous procession of coaches left Austria to meet the French royal family; she would never see her homeland again. Aged 14, she was off to a new life, one where childhood pursuits would be forgotten and she would become, for better or worse, an icon of royal opulence.

The journey was arduous and long but, on 14 May, the young newlyweds finally laid eyes on one another for the first time. In a forest clearing near Compiegne, Marie Antoinette threw herself at the feet of her new husband and his grandfather, King Louis XV, declaring her devotion to them. The young dauphin gently raised his wife to stand and escorted her to his carriage, in which she made the remainder of the journey to Versailles.

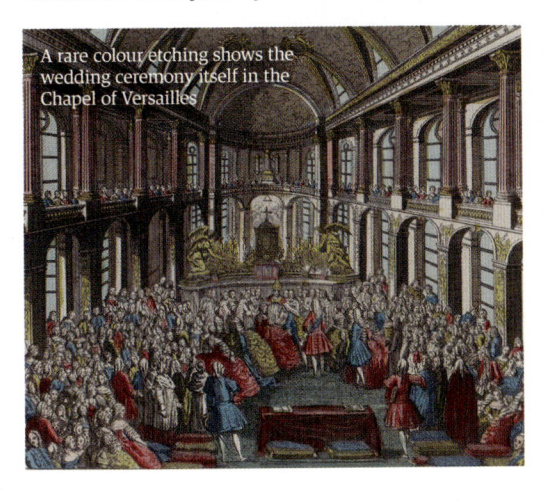

A rare colour etching shows the wedding ceremony itself in the Chapel of Versailles

The religious ceremony on 16 May was a dazzling affair. It was held in the glittering splendour of the royal chapel of Versailles and Marie Antoinette's dress must have been magnificent. No expense was spared - it was made of cloth of silver and decorated with pearls and precious stones, dazzling beneath the palace chandeliers. Although no pictures or fragments exist for us to marvel at today, society wedding gowns from the time give just a hint of how fabulous a creation it would have been. Unfortunately, Marie Antoinette had been measured for the gown months earlier and when it came to lace her into it, no amount of corsetry or willpower could make up for the fact that the ill-fitting dress just wouldn't fasten. Even with the laces at their tightest, the gown gaped open at the back and exposed the dauphine's shift to the illustrious crowd who had gathered to watch.

Though some of the wedding guests laughed behind their hands at the unthinkable sartorial blunder, the wedding was a roaring success. A crowd of 5,000 crammed into grandstands in the Hall of Mirrors and the cream of European society watched the procession pass by, witnessing the dawn of one of the most famous and iconic marriages in royal history.

BAD OMENS

For all its pomp and splendour, the day was plagued with events that were seen as ill omens, the first of which was the ill-fitting gown. Worse, when Marie Antoinette sat down to sign the marriage register, a blot of ink dripped onto the page and obscured part of her name. On the wedding day a storm raged that was fierce enough to cancel planned public celebrations, battering the palace walls and windows. When a fete was eventually held weeks later, strong winds and fireworks resulted in an inferno that claimed many lives.

Still, the day itself was hailed as a great occasion, and after a day of feasting and parties, the newlyweds were escorted in time-honoured tradition to the marital bed. Here they fell into an exhausted slumber, with the business of producing an heir left for another time, far in the future.

43

How to GET A BAROQUE HAIRSTYLE

Dress your hair in a coiffure that turns heads, like the it-girls in Versailles

In the 18th century, more was more. Extravagance was the leading principle in art, music, architecture and, of course, fashion. Seldom have hairstyles been so wonderful and fantastic as during the Baroque period.

Ladies all over Europe wanted to imitate the elaborate styles of the French court, which took inspiration from everything from political alliance to major life events.

While the likes of Madam de Pompadour would employ a team of servants to create her giant coiffures, beauty blogger Lucy Kyselica explains how you can do it yourself. For more of her historic style tips, visit **loepsie.com**.

Apply a pomade
Prepare a mixture of beef marrow or lard, hazelnut oil and a few drops of lemon essence to set the hair.

Style scaffold
Use wool, tow, a wire frame, or whatever bulky material you deem appropriate to enlarge the hairstyle.

Seek assistance
To reach maximum height, request help from a professional and provide them with a step-stool for better access.

The powder machine
Use this bellows-like device to blow an even amount of powder onto the hair for a fashionable look.

WHAT YOU'LL NEED...
- POMADE
- POWDER
- CUSHION
- CURLING IRON
- ACCESSORIES

1. CURL AND ROLL
Divide your hair into front and back sections by parting it parallel to the face, about two inches in and down just behind the ears. Split the front hair into two-inch sections and coat each in a good amount of pomade, then apply powder. Curl the section with a heated curling iron, roll it up and pin above the hairline. Repeat with all of the front hair.

2. FRIZZ YOUR HAIR
Separate the remaining hair in two. Tie the back section away. Going by two-inch sections again, frizz the front hair by coating it with sufficient pomade and powder, and back-combing it. Hold the hair firmly away from the head and press the comb towards the head so that the hair forms a mat and stands upright.

How to get a Baroque hairstyle

HOW NOT TO... MAINTAIN PERSONAL HYGIENE

In 1768, a letter appeared in *The London Magazine* in which a young man expressed his concern for the health of women after having witnessed the undressing of his elderly aunt's hair. When the hair dresser "opened her head", as he called it, the gentleman was met by an incredible stench caused by layers of pomade, powder and sweat, which had been confined in the coiffure for nine weeks. The smell was bad enough but there was more.

As the hair was being combed out, swarms of little bugs could be seen frantically running around in different directions. The hairdresser assured the gentleman that the bugs couldn't spread to different parts of the body, for they were unable to break through the barrier of powder and pomade.

The greatly disturbed gentleman published this graphic description in an attempt to restore ladies' former cleanliness — it had no effect.

3 — PIN CUSHION
Place an arrowhead-shaped cushion in the centre of the frizzed hair. You can now pin the frizzed hair to the cushion from all sides, securing the hairstyle and reaching the desired shape. Make sure that the cushion is thoroughly covered and disappears into the style — it will help support a hat or accessory later on.

4 — STYLE YOUR STRANDS
Starting above the ear, unpin a curl. Coat it with pomade and powder, and frizz it thoroughly. Smooth the outside of the strand and roll it towards the scalp so that it forms a little egg. Repeat to form three curls on each side. Frizz the remaining hair, pin it to the cushion on top and smooth down the front.

5 — PLAIT TO FINISH
Untie the back hair, comb it well and coat it with pomade and powder. Create one curl on the side of the neck, which will hang down gracefully over the shoulder. Plait the rest of the hair before pulling it up and pinning it to the cushion. Spread out the plait by gently tugging at the sides to make it wider.

6 — ACCESSORISE
We're almost there! Protect your face with a powdering cone and ask someone to blow powder onto your coiffure using the powder machine. Make sure you get a nice even coating. If needed, fill any gaps using a powdered swan-down puff. Lastly, accessorise your do using pearls, ribbons, feathers, silk flowers or an evening bonnet. Et voilà, you're done!

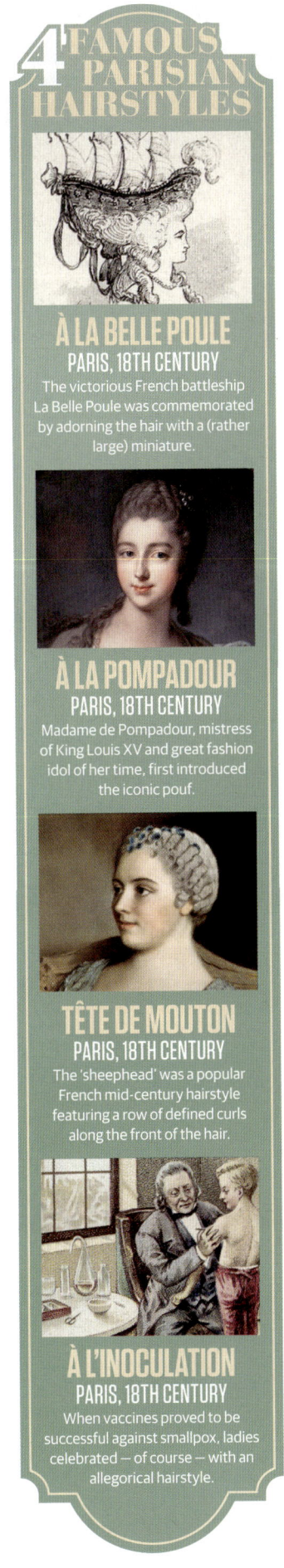

---

4 FAMOUS PARISIAN HAIRSTYLES

À LA BELLE POULE
PARIS, 18TH CENTURY
The victorious French battleship La Belle Poule was commemorated by adorning the hair with a (rather large) miniature.

À LA POMPADOUR
PARIS, 18TH CENTURY
Madame de Pompadour, mistress of King Louis XV and great fashion idol of her time, first introduced the iconic pouf.

TÊTE DE MOUTON
PARIS, 18TH CENTURY
The 'sheephead' was a popular French mid-century hairstyle featuring a row of defined curls along the front of the hair.

À L'INOCULATION
PARIS, 18TH CENTURY
When vaccines proved to be successful against smallpox, ladies celebrated — of course — with an allegorical hairstyle.

45

46

EAST meets WEST

Western fashion does not exist in a vacuum; for centuries, it has been influenced by global culture and has, in turn, influenced other cultures too

Written by Catherine Curzon

Depicted by artist Alfred Stevens, a Western woman wears a blue floral Japanese kimono

For centuries, as the world has opened up, Western fashion has been influenced by many different cultures, as European and American consumers began to absorb garments, tradition, techniques, patterns and more. These influences began to enter Western fashion in earnest in the 17th and 18th centuries, when exploration and trade expansion saw travellers journey further across the globe than ever before. On the far side of the earth they experienced new worlds and cultures, far removed from those they had left behind.

Clothing that seemed impossibly exotic caught the imagination of fashionistas in the West, who were keen to appropriate elements of this dress and assimilate it into existing styles. For those who were living overseas, 'going native' and dressing entirely in the attire of the country one was visiting was frowned on, but taking elements of that culture to enhance one's own wardrobe and home was considered not only fair game, but practically cutting edge. Much of this, of course, was done with little care or understanding; instead, Westerners cherry-picked the elements they liked, rejecting or refashioning those they didn't.

Perhaps more than any other country, China had long fascinated the West, having been closed to Western traders from the 14th century to the 17th. When trade routes reopened, European travellers flooded into the country and there they found Chinese silk that was quite unlike that in use back home, thanks to a variety of dyes and weaving and pattern techniques unique to China. They exported Chinese silk to the West in vast amounts and charged a premium for it, leading to a fascination with the weaving, needlework and intricate hand-painting techniques employed by the Chinese silk workers. Rather than use the silk in the creation of Chinese garments, however, it was instead adapted into Western garments, leading to the juxtaposition of traditional gowns decorated with intricate Chinese symbolism and scenes. Gowns or menswear that utilised Chinese silk was a mark of wealth and status in society. It was a clear indication that the wearer had the money to purchase a textile that had been imported from the other side of the globe and have it created into garments that were the height of European fashion.

Of course, it wasn't only textiles that found their way from China to the West. Specific elements of Chinese dress began to appear on Western clothing too, suggesting that the wearer was someone who took an interest in the world at large and was up

Paul Poiret's use of the turban, as depicted by artist Georges Lepape

"Clothing that seemed exotic caught the imagination of fashionistas in the West"

Famed for her love of Turkish dress, Lady Mary Wortley Montagu caused a fashion sensation

East meets West

ABOVE Wax prints have become a cultural staple for some African women

RIGHT Empress Joséphine loved the Indian Kashmir shawl; here she wears one shawl with a dress made from another

CULTURAL APPROPRIATION

For centuries, Western fashion simply adopted Eastern culture, with few trying to understand it

Cultural appropriation is the inappropriate or unacknowledged adoption of elements of one culture by members of another, which is typically more dominant. Accusations of cultural appropriation have long since dogged the fashion industry and continue to do so to this day. From fashionable Regency dandies relaxing in turbans amid imported Indian décor and furniture to ladies wearing gowns made of Chinese silk that carried symbols of which they had no understanding, overseas cultures were simply seen as a commodity to be sold.

Cultural appropriation did not, however, end in the 19th century, but continued into the modern era as major fashion houses in the last hundred years have borrowed styles and patterns from cultures that have gone unacknowledged. Today, however, there is a pushback against this appropriation and lack of acknowledgement. Once, Western women wore cheongsams and pushed chopsticks into their hair, but no more. In 2018, Gucci's decision to showcase white models wearing $800 turbans on the runway saw them fiercely criticised by Sikh groups in an echo of the controversy that hit Victoria's Secret when lingerie-clad models walked in Native American war bonnets.

Today, campaigns are underway that seek to decolonise fashion, highlighting just how much Western design takes non-Western concepts and uses them freely, without any acknowledgement. More and more, creators from different cultural backgrounds are showcasing their own authentic pieces, created from their lived experiences and imbued with their own cultures. Fashion has a long way to go, but it has at least made a start.

In 2012, Victora's Secret attracted criticism when models walked the runway in Native American war bonnets

---

to the minute when it came to fashion. Among these was the button knot, a knot which was traditionally worn as a button on undergarments and nightclothes, as it was more comfortable than a traditional hard button. Though a workaday item in China, to the Western eye they were eye-poppingly exotic, and they became a popular decorative choice. Also absorbed from Chinese culture was frogging, an ornamental closure that would be fastened with a decorative button knot. Though frogging had already been adopted from the Hungarian Hussars into European military uniform, it became a popular closure on the banyan, itself adopted from India.

India played a significant role in the meeting of Eastern and Western fashion, both as a major supplier of textiles, such as muslin, cotton and wool, but also in one very specific garment that entered Western fashion as an enduring favourite. This was the Indian house gown, which became hugely fashionable in the West as the 18th-century banyan, an often opulent, always comfortable robe in which men would lounge while relaxing at home. Untailored and loose-fitting, the banyan was a startling development in the rigid-tailored world of the upper-class Georgians. Often decorated in patterns borrowed from India, such as paisley, or other flamboyant designs borrowed from the East, they became a central part of a fashionable gentleman's wardrobe. Today, the spirit of the banyan still exists as the dressing gown; paisley, of course, remains a traditional favourite. Napoleon's wife, Joséphine, meanwhile, was devoted to her Indian Kashmir shawl, starting a trend for the pashmina that exploded all over again in the 1990s.

From the 16th century until the 18th, Turquerie was a fashionable craze that saw the wealthy embrace all things Ottoman. Fashionable tastemakers were painted wearing Turkish-inspired dress and surrounded by Ottoman furnishings and antiques and nobody did more to popularise this style than Lady Mary Wortley Montagu, the medical pioneer and author. As wife to the ambassador, Montagu arrived in Turkey in 1717 and sent back long descriptions of the clothing she found there and which she quickly adopted; in

49

In the 1920s, flappers embraced Tutmania, echoing ancient Egypt in their clothes, hair and make-up

EGYPTIENNES

TUTMANIA

Though Westerners had long been fascinated with Egypt, the discovery of Tutankhamun's tomb sent fashionistas into overdrive

Egypt had not been immune from Western appropriation over the years, but it received a whole new lease of life in 1922, when Howard Carter led the excavation of the tomb of Tutankhamun, which had lain undiscovered for more than 3,000 years.

Ancient Egypt had initially become fashionable in the late-18th century when Napoleon attempted to occupy the country, but in the 1920s, it seized fashion and wouldn't let go. Loose flapper dresses, echoing the shifts worn in Egypt, became the must-have for fashionable women about town and these were often decorated with symbols appropriated from Egypt, including scarab beetles, lotus flowers, solar discs and more, while textile manufacturers sought to recreate the hues found in the tomb. Short, bobbed hair was the on-trend cut and black kohl eyeliner, which echoed that seen in depictions of ancient Egypt and that on Tutankhamun's death mask, became the cutting edge of modern fashion.

It wasn't only clothes that the long-dead pharaoh inspired, either; hats and elaborately beaded evening headdresses went on sale that showcased motifs found in the tomb. For those who wanted something a little more subtle, there was even a walking cane on which the handle was the head of an ibis. At the showier end of the spectrum, meanwhile, jewellers offered dazzling pieces that sought to echo Tutankhamun's finery. Cartier, a name synonymous with luxury, created a gold brooch in the form of a winged scarab, studded with priceless stones. What Tutankhamun would've made of it is anyone's guess.

fact, Lady Mary was painted in Turkish dress, her stays cast off as she lounged in comfort. Her letters, which are a fascinating glimpse into a privileged life, were shared widely in England and fanned the flames on the fascination with Turquerie.

For those who didn't want to commit to the full dress as Lady Mary did, elements of Ottoman dress were brought into Western fashion in the forms of tassels and textiles, while all forms of foreign dress became popular and stylish choices for upper-class masques. However, the influence of Eastern fashion on the West didn't end in the 18th century. In the mid-1800s, Japan suddenly opened to international trade after 250 years of isolation, leading to an explosion in Western excitement for all things Japanese. It was reciprocated, as the Japanese excitedly embraced Western culture in turn.

Just as in India, where British colonial rule had seen Western dress become an everyday sight, in 1870s Japan, courtiers and government officials working with Western nations wore Western dress. Yet the tide flowed both ways, with Westerners

Fashionable Georgian gentlemen embraced the banyan, lounging at home in a garment borrowed from India

ABOVE Though the Chinese government ruled that trousers be worn with the cheongsam, women had other ideas

BELOW Items such as this turban, designed by Paul Poiret in 1911, borrowed liberally from other cultures

East meets West

This Chinese button knot and frogging demonstrates how ornate this simple fastening could become

From 1923-24, this evening dress by Callot Soeurs emphasises their fascination with both the beauty of Chinese textiles and the simplicity of the lines

"To some, Western dress was a sign of modernity or a symbol of wealth"

in India often wearing Indian garments to relax at home; though this was less common in Japan, there were some who mounted an enthusiastic defence of the comfort of traditional Japanese dress versus that of the Westerner. For most, however, elements were there to be absorbed, so Paul Poiret accessorised his looks with a turban, while Callot Soeurs embraced Chinese textiles and motifs in the fashion-forward 1920s. Throughout the 1930s, Chinese and Japanese influences could be seen, embracing the fascination with the mysterious East.

While much of the story of East meets West in fashion is very much the former servicing the latter, this isn't always the case. During the 19th century, Dutch merchants introduced the people of West and Central Africa to wax prints, which have become a staple of African dress. These prints began during the Dutch colonisation of Indonesia, when Dutch merchants first encountered batik, which they began mass-producing in the Netherlands. They hoped that the industrial manufacturing process, which simplified the complicated process of creating patterns in the cloth using melted wax and dye, would overtake traditional production methods and outsell handmade batik.

However, the Indonesian people found the cloth inferior to their traditionally produced original and the market for the Dutch version was poor. Seeking a new market, traders loaded the batik onto their ships and carried it to Africa, where they found a receptive audience. Wax prints became hugely popular and developed into an artform all their own, by which African women could communicate messages to their peers. By the 20th century, the majority of prints were made by African people and the industry continues to thrive today.

Of course, it doesn't stop there; the Nehru jacket, which became popular in the West in the second half of the 20th century, was influenced by the Indian achkan worn by Indian prime minister Jawaharlal Nehru. The hip-length tailored garment with a mandarin collar is not, however, a true reflection of those worn by Nehru, which reached the knees. However, when the jacket was embraced by Western mods, it had become considerably shorter.

Similarly, the cheongsam is considered by many to be the classic Chinese dress, but this fitted gown owes more to the 20th century than centuries past. While the cheongsam developed from the qipao, the robes worn by women of the Manchu people, the founders of the Qing dynasty, in the 17th century, the dress as it exists today actually incorporates a huge amount of Western influence. Fitted, fashionable and daring, the cheongsam enjoyed massive popularity among the wealthy in China from the 1920s to the 1960s, where it served as a symbol of the new Republic. Women wore their dresses shorter and shorter, cutting the slits higher and fitting them more closely than ever, emulating the new freedom enjoyed by flappers in the West. In 1929, the cheongsam became one of China's national dresses, though the government decreed that it must be worn with trousers and reach the calf. Suffice to say, Chinese women paid no attention to the new ruling.

Over the 20th century, Western clothing became ever more dominant, often replacing traditional forms of dress that had existed for centuries. To some, Western dress was a sign of modernity or even a symbol of wealth, while for others, particularly the young, it was a rebellion against all that had gone before. However, not every culture and person has succumbed; while Western fashion has become dominant, it will never replace traditional dress.

Today, fashion continues to be a conversation between cultures, exchanging inspiration and ideas both on the catwalk and the high street. Though new inspiration no longer comes from cultures that have been isolated for decades, it instead comes from designers who carry their identity in their blood and who have been influenced not only by their own upbringing and culture, but by that of their forebears too. It is just one more reason why the language of fashion continues to evolve, telling stories about not only the clothes themselves, but the designers who create them, the people who wear them and the worlds that inspired them.

DROP DEAD *Gorgeous*

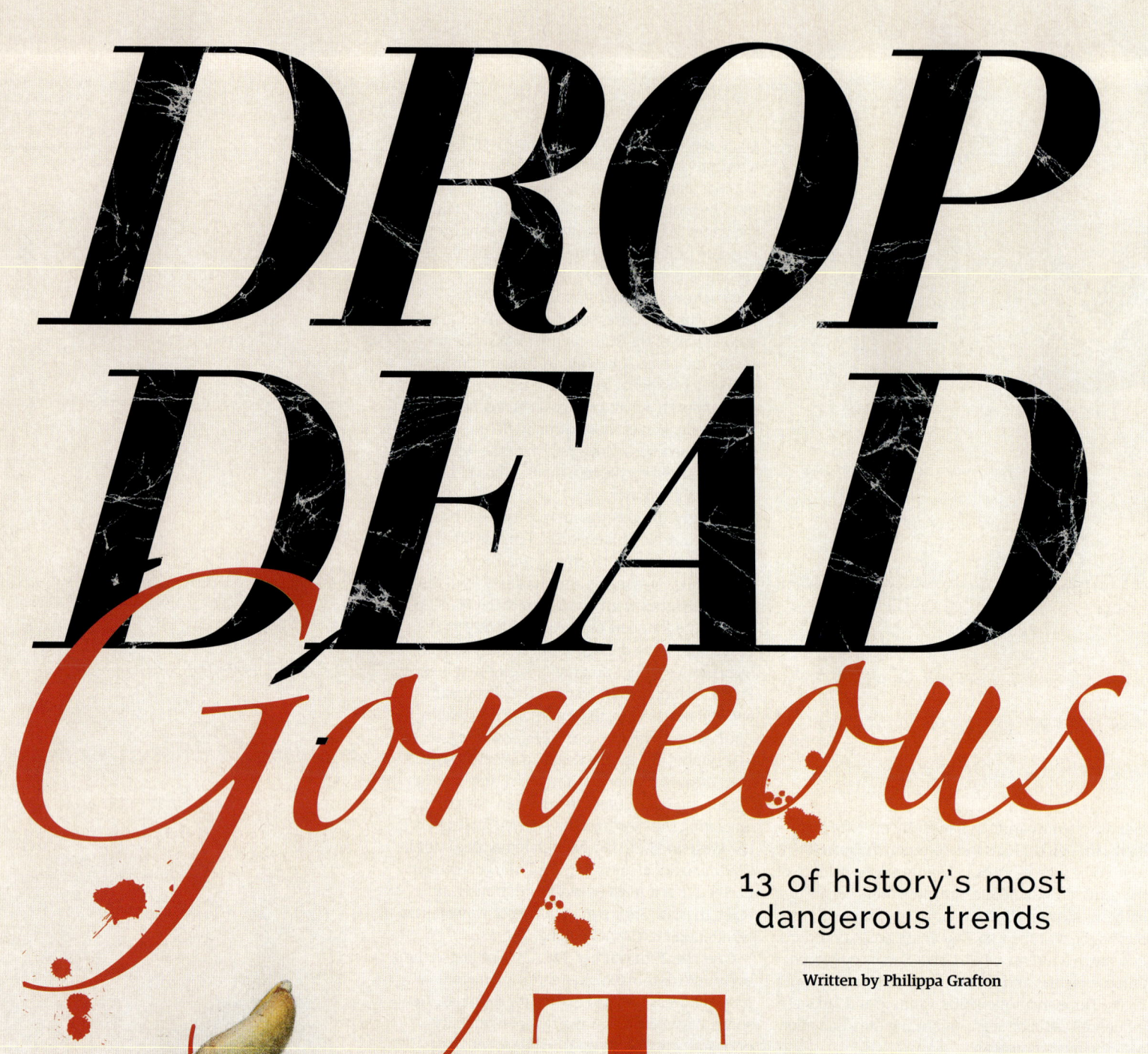

13 of history's most dangerous trends

Written by Philippa Grafton

The lengths we go to for beauty know no bounds: plastic surgery, chemical peels and tattooed make-up are all extreme measures to achieve that picture-perfect look, but at least we've got our doctor's seal of approval on their safety status. Beauty addicts from years gone by weren't so lucky. From skin regimens brimming with poisons and parasite-based diets to breathtakingly tight corsets and the hottest hairstyles, discover the 13 deadliest trends that claimed their very own fashion victims.

Drop dead gorgeous

CORSETS

The fatal finery of choice in the 19th century, corsets already had a bad reputation in the 1800s, with doctors frowning upon them and a plethora of literature condemning the undergarment – in 1848, one doctor even suggested that wearing a corset was akin to committing suicide. To achieve the hourglass figure so popular at the time, women's corsets would be laced as tightly as possible, with the recommended waist size set to 18 inches.

Wearing their corsets, ladies often experienced headaches, breathing trouble and fainting. That was just the tip of the iceberg, however – there were widespread reports of broken ribs, and extreme lacing led to displaced internal organs, deformed rib cages and even death.

OF CORSETS NOT BAD FOR YOU!

As well as stopping the wearer from breathing properly, corsets could affect internal organs

Nature versus Corsets, Illustrated.

TIME TO DITCH THE BRONZER!

LEAD MAKE-UP

For centuries, it was deemed the height of fashion to have pale skin; tanned, freckled faces were considered improper and a sign of being a peasant. Women – as well as men – would go to extreme lengths to keep their faces as white as possible, using pastes, powders and potions. The key ingredient in many of these lotions was lead.

Using lead-based make-up led to baldness and inflamed skin, and then a vicious cycle, where disguising skin defects meant using even more lead make-up. Accidental inhalation of lead-based powders, however, proved catastrophic. Even worse than the physical side effects was the psychological damage that lead poisoning triggered, including destroying the nervous system, causing paralysis and brain damage. Lead palsy was a common symptom of poisoning, which is characterised by a dropped wrist and localised paralysis of the hands.

Worst of all, if you think the days of lead in make-up have passed, think again. A recent discovery found that hundreds of lipsticks across the world were contaminated with lead, but luckily the amount is so low that it shouldn't affect you – assuming you don't buy lipsticks to eat, of course.

CRINOLINE SKIRTS

In the 19th century, the epitome of elegance for women was to dramatically distort their natural body shape by wearing a crinoline skirt - a hooped petticoat that was as large as reasonably possible. Almost two-metre-wide skirts might have been the height of fashion, but they came with a host of problems, from the dull to outright dangerous.

Perhaps the most common problem caused by the hooped skirt was the sheer amount of space it took up. Ladies could fit through doors, but that was about the extent of their usefulness. At social events, the skirts were horribly impractical - one contemporary criticised them by claiming that one woman in her skirt took up the space of three men. Sadly, that wasn't the extent of the dangers of crinoline skirts. Being as popular among the lower classes as the wealthy, factory owners were dismayed to find that their female employees were wearing crinoline to work. Stories of women being dragged into machinery plagued 19th-century newspapers, as well as those of unsuspecting fashionistas being blown to their deaths in strong, windy conditions and caught under carriage wheels.

Worst of all, however, was the disturbingly common death by fire. The skirts were highly flammable and, with the ladies unaware of their proximity to a candle or fireplace, would often go up in flames. In Chile in 1863, up to 3,000 people died in a church fire that has been blamed in part on the flammability of the skirts and the fact that they blocked the exits.

THIS SEASON'S HOTTEST LOOK

Steel cage crinolines were some of the most popular, but they could also be made from other materials including whalebone

OWN THE DANCE FLOOR

At their most ridiculous, crinoline skirts could be more than five metres wide

FLAMMABLE HAIRSTYLES

TOWERING UPDOS

The trend for tall tresses took off in the late-18th century, with women using hair cushions and false hair to reach dizzying heights. However, forgetful of the towering tinder atop their heads, many ladies would be set alight by chandeliers and candles. If they didn't burn to death, they often died of exposure or shock.

COMBUSTIBLE COMBS

Imitating the look of ivory, celluloid became a popular material used for fashion accessories in the early-20th century, but the danger it posed to workers and wearers alike was deadly, as it was explosive. Once ignited, it would combust in a ball of fire and release toxic gases. If the fire didn't kill you, the fumes would.

HAIR SPRAY HORROR

With perfectly coiffed tresses being the height of fashion and the hairstyle of choice for many, the 1950s saw the invention of hair spray to help keep curls fixed in their place. However, the key ingredient in all hair sprays - vinyl chloride monomer - proved to be not only highly flammable but also toxic.

Drop dead gorgeous

RADIOACTIVE SKIN CREAM

In their quest for a face with that youthful healthy 'glow', the women of the 20th century began smothering their faces in radioactive creams. For a fresh-faced, radiant complexion, many women of the interwar period turned to lotions that were made with radium – so radioactive it glows in the dark. Of all the sellers of radioactive creams, a French brand named Tho-Radia topped the charts with their radium-thorium recipe. With their range of creams, toothpastes and cosmetics, women applied radioactive make-up on a daily basis. As you'd expect, radiation poisoning and cancer figures soared.

MERCURY HATS

GO CRAZY FOR FELT!

Women weren't the only fashion victims in history. While different types of men's hats came and went in and out of fashion, one element endured the test of time: mercury. It was this ingredient in the making of hats that earned hatters their 'mad' reputation. Using mercury to turn fur into felt, the process would release noxious fumes that could kill. Symptoms would start innocently enough – hands shook and trembled, teeth came loose and the hatter became unco-ordinated. The next stage was much more tragic, with symptoms such as severe memory loss, anxiety, depression and hallucinations. Poisoned by mercury, the nervous system would slowly collapse, seeing a victim fall into a coma and in extreme cases, leading to death.

By World War II, the use of mercury in hat-making was banned, though it wasn't down to health reasons. In fact, the mercury was needed for detonators.

DEADLY NIGHTSHADE EYE DROPS

The deadly nightshade drops caused the user's eyes to dilate

Sickly sweet and toxic to the touch, deadly nightshade could be found in most Roman women's beauty regimen. Also known as belladonna ('beautiful woman' in Italian), the poisonous plant was distilled into eye drops that gave the user that classic, sexy doe-eyed look. Too strong a mix, however, and they would go blind. Accidentally ingest some, and they could expect extreme hallucinations, brain damage and death.

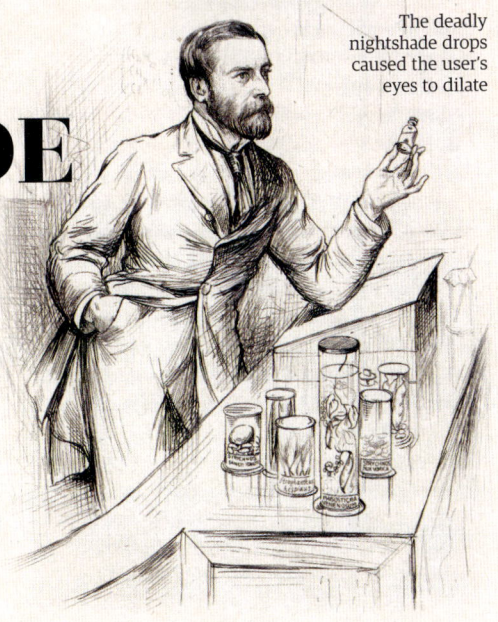

REVOLTING REMEDIES

If beauty wasn't lethal, then it was sure to be repulsive. Discover some of the most questionable treatments from years gone by

LARD HAIR PRODUCTS

Dull, lifeless hair bringing you down? Try our 18th century wigs, sculpted with the finest lard. Cages to deter mice from nesting in lard-soaked wig sold separately.

MOUSE FUR EYEBROWS

Do your eyebrows leave a lot to be desired? Head in store now to pick up your own fair trade, organic mouse fur eyebrows, and get a **FREE** fitting session. Based on an original 18th century design.

BEETLE BLOOD LIPSTICK

Channel your inner Cleopatra and embrace your secret Elizabeth I with this innovative blend of crushed carmine beetles and ants for rich, red lips.

URINE MOUTHWASH

Formulated with the finest Portuguese piddle, this brand-new mouthwash is guaranteed to freshen your breath and leave him longing for more. It worked for the Romans!

CROCODILE DUNG FACE MASK

This isn't just any crocodile dung face mask – this is an all-natural, full-bodied, youth-preserving crocodile dung face mask, served precisely mixed with the finest mud. Based on an Ancient Greek recipe.

SANDPAPER SMOOTHER

Take inspiration from the 40s and banish unsightly hairs with this hair exfoliator you'll find in your hubby's toolbox! Simply rub sandpaper following the grain for legs as smooth as marble.

* CALL NOW *

FOOT BINDING

Feet: you either love them or you loathe them. Whether you harbour a soft spot for the sight of twinkling toes or the thought of feet makes your skin crawl, foot binding was a trend that took China by storm for more than a millennium. Those sensitive about feet, look away now.

Popular during the Song dynasty (10th-13th century), women with bound feet were considered the height of elegance. To achieve the look, the process began early for girls - between the ages of two and seven - while their feet were supple and soft, and their minds blissfully unaware of the pain they were about to experience. Next, all their toes - but excluding the big toes, thankfully - would be broken and folded down into the ball of the foot. Next, the arch would be bent to its extreme, then the foot would be bound in the tightest cloth. From here, years of tight binding would ensure that the foot wouldn't grow to an unsightly size.

The cruel practice would cut off circulation in the toes, which more often than not led to infections and gangrene. Feet would be covered in sores and often gave off a foul stench - all the better to be covered up with elegant little silk shoes, then.

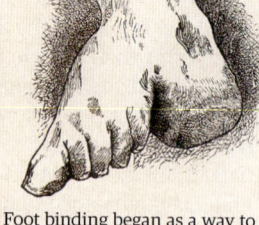

Foot binding began as a way to display status, as wealthy women did not need their feet to work

STIFF COLLARS

BREATHTAKING!

Championed as the 'father killer', the detachable stiff collar for men was just as dangerous as any of its female counterparts. Popular in the 19th century, the stiff collar could be attached to a shirt with studs. Highly starched, it gripped the man's throat in its cotton-y vice, with its point jutting up into the windpipe. Under normal, sober conditions, the collar could be quite constrictive but otherwise harmless. When a man fell into a post-dinner drunken stupor, however, the stiff collar would claim its victim. As a man sat in his armchair and his head dropped to his chest, the collar could block the windpipe and stop the blood flow through the carotid arteries. As he slept, he could be suffocated by his own collar.

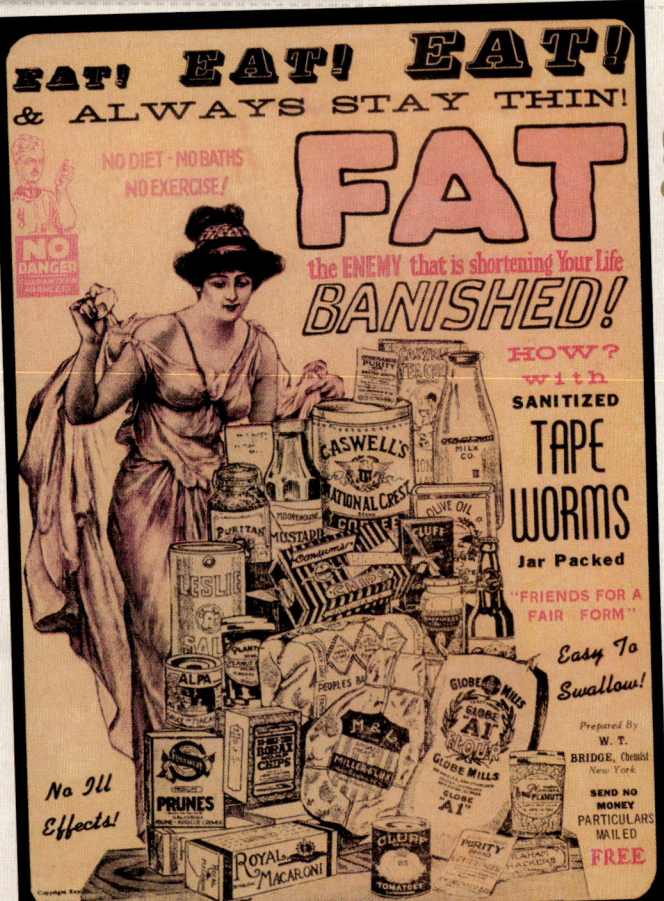

TAPEWORM DIET

EWWWWW!

Tapeworms can grow up to six metres long

Feeling fat, but not willing to exercise or embrace a healthier diet? Tapeworms are sure to solve the problem. In the early 20th century, tapeworms and tapeworm eggs were sold in jars and as pills as a form of dieting. Simply consume your tapeworms, wait for them to absorb your food, then - once you're down to your ideal weight - take an anti-parasitic tablet. Results were guaranteed with the tapeworm diet, but it came with a host of terrible side-effects, including cysts in the brain, spinal cord and eyes, meningitis and epilepsy. Maybe stick to the celery sticks…

56

Drop dead gorgeous

ARSENIC DRESSES

Make-up might have been deadly, but the silent killer of the 19th century was the arsenic-infused dress. The discovery of Scheele's Green dye in the late-18th century was a revelation to the fashion world – previously unattainable, this new shade turned the most bland dresses a vibrant, enduring green. The downside? It was fatally poisonous. Made from copper arsenite, the dye was found in everything - from dresses and wallpapers to sweets – with disastrous consequences.

Wearers of coveted green gowns would find themselves developing nasty rashes and wart-like growths on their skin, but the workers creating the garments suffered the most from the effects of arsenic poisoning. Inhaling the dye as it wafted around the workshop, seamstresses were the real victims. Starting with headaches, they'd soon experience cramps, convulsions, visual impairment, followed by coma and death.

Worst of all, Scheele's Green might have earned itself a bad reputation, but in actuality arsenic could be found in many other dyes too – even the most plain dress could become a dress to die for.

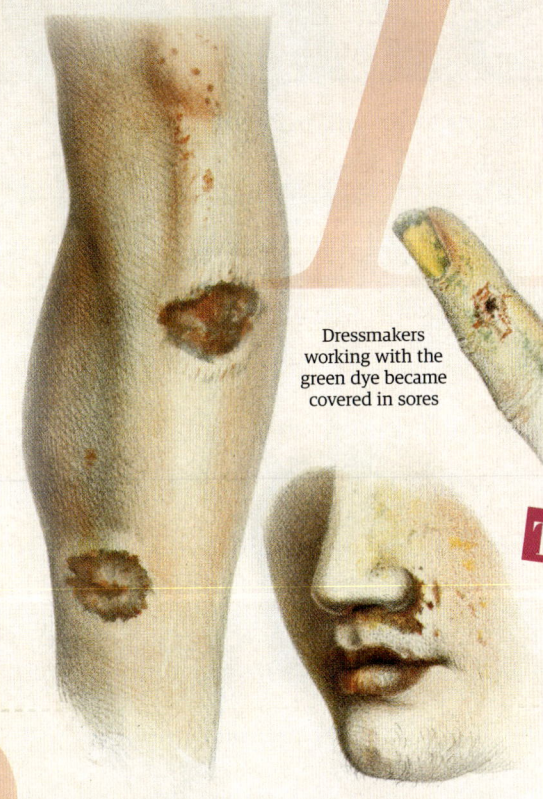

Dressmakers working with the green dye became covered in sores

A DRESS TO DIE FOR

LICE-INFECTED WIGS

The 18th century marked the heyday of the powdered wig, with men and women alike eschewing their natural locks for a more extravagant coiffure. Men often opted for a full wig, known as a peruke, to conceal any baldness, while women would use partial wigs to add to their natural hair in order to create excessive, ornate styles. The pros of wigs were many: as well as hiding baldness, wigs gave the illusion of youth and required next to no upkeep. On the flip side, wig-wearers had to bear the brunt of sores on the head. Lice was a serious issue for women, too – extravagant styles were not just expensive, but took hours to construct, and women would keep them for weeks on end to justify the expense. Unable to reach into their luxurious locks, ladies would have to use rods to scratch their heads, or risk being eaten alive by their hair-dwelling enemies.

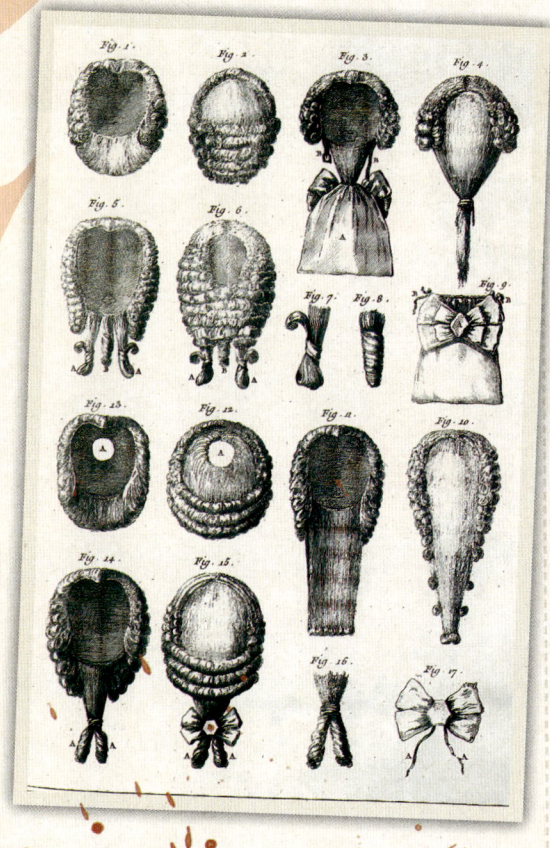

X-RAY HAIR REMOVAL

Upon the discovery of X-rays for hair removal, a fervour swept through beauty circles. In 1924, Albert C Geyser invented the infamous Tricho System – a method of removing hair with X-rays marketed as "harmless" and "infallible". This cure for unwanted hair turned out to be more dangerous than anyone could have imagined. Hair loss may have been immediate, but wrinkling soon followed, along with mottling, atrophy and ulcerations. The Tricho System was abandoned in 1932, but its side effects on former clients were by no means over. Years later, patients found themselves with cancerous tumours, with over a third of radiation-induced cancer linked back to X-ray hair removal.

57

FASHION and the INDUSTRIAL REVOLUTION

The Industrial Revolution ushered in a whole new era of fashion, changing that rarefied world forever

Written by Catherine Curzon

Fashion and the Industrial Revolution

Once upon a time, the United Kingdom was a world of cottage industries, just as it had been for centuries; there was no large-scale industrial production and manufacture, but small-scale manufacturers, working precisely as quickly as one person could. The vast majority of manufacturing was done by hand and rural and agricultural industries dominated, but from the mid-18th century, all of that was set to change. In the race for mass production at low cost, humans became second to machines, necessary only to ensure that the machines never stopped.

As the British Empire began to expand across the globe, it brought with it an increased demand for goods that could simply not be met by such small-scale methods of production. Technological growth was necessary, and, in the textile industry, which was one of the nation's most valuable, it came swiftly. Traditionally, cloth and yarn was produced by spinners and weavers, often working from the homes. Many of these were family businesses, with children washing and carding, women spinning the yarn on a spinning wheel and men weaving the cloth on a loom. However, once the Industrial Revolution began, these family businesses were soon wiped out.

> "In the race for mass production, humans became second to machines, necessary only to ensure that the machines never stopped"

One of the first developments that led the way to mass production was John Kay's 1733 invention, the flying shuttle. On previous looms, the shuttle was thrown through the threads by hand, but Kay automated the process, mounting the shuttle on wheels and using paddles to move the shuttle from side to side. It allowed fabrics to be woven far more quickly, especially wide pieces, which would previously have required at least two weavers.

In 1764, meanwhile, James Hargreaves' spinning jenny revolutionised the spinning of raw materials such as flax, cotton and wool, into thread. For centuries, this had been done on a spinning wheel, but the spinning jenny put eight spindles

A linen mill in Ireland bleaches its fabrics in the sun

Inside a sizing room, where cotton fibres were starched and strengthened before being sent to looms

into one machine, all controlled by a single wheel and belt. This meant that it could do the work of eight people, though this number increased with subsequent generations of the machine until as many as 120 spindles could operate at once. Suddenly, yarn was available in vast amounts, laying the foundations for large-scale textile production to begin.

Five years later Richard Arkwright unveiled his water frame, an industrial spinning machine powered by water. The frame could spin nearly 100 threads, 24 hours a day, but required mills to be built near a water source. Watt's steam engine of 1776, however, meant that machines could run anywhere. Vast factories were opened that contained floor after floor of heavy machinery, with workers tending the machines that were doing the work that had once been theirs.

The spinning mule, Samuel Crompton's 1879 invention, brought together elements of other machines to create a revolutionary moment in the industrialisation of textiles. The spinning mule could produce more thread than ever before. This was followed by Edward Cartwright's power loom in 1785, which automated the entire weaving process, reducing human involvement even more. These industrial developments put an end to the cottage industry of textile production, destroying what had once been one of the nation's most important small sectors. Now production could happen on a vast scale in enormous mills, where workers were needed not for their experience and expertise, but to service and ensure the running of the machines.

> "These industrial developments put an end to the cottage industry of textile production"

Mass manufacture put fashion in everyone's reach, but couturiers such as the House of Worth still offered handmade luxury

Vast factories such as Cromford Mill were constructed specifically to house the machines that would revolutionise the textile industry

60

Fashion and the Industrial Revolution

Women working at the machines in a textile factory

With each new technological development, the textile industry took another leap away from the cottage industry it had been for so long and as it did, the roles of men and women in the process changed. Though small-scale spinning using individual wheels had traditionally been women's work, the operation of machines such as the mule needed brute force, so they became the responsibility of men. With the men working the mules, women began to operate the looms instead, which required less physical strength. Children, meanwhile, went to work in the mills too, scurrying between looms to clear waste or loosen blockages. The work was hard, dangerous and unforgiving.

One of the most important developments in the history and democratisation of fashion was the widespread adoption of the sewing machine. Though specialist machines had been available for several decades, they didn't reach mass popularity until 1846 when Elias Howe unveiled his sewing machine to the public. The machine stitched and interlocked but, despite being very popular, was not the only option. The popularity of Howe's machine was overtaken by that of Isaac Merritt Singer, America's largest manufacturer of sewing machines.

The advent of the sewing machine changed fashion forever. Clothing manufacturers brought them up in huge numbers and launched the very first "ready to wear" lines. The sewing machine was the beginning of true mass manufacturing of fashion itself, putting brand new, mass-produced and affordable garments in the reach of almost all consumers for the very first time. Suddenly, virtually everything was affordable, and clothing manufacturers could afford to innovate and experiment. With production times faster than ever before and a huge choice of materials available at affordable prices, designers let their imaginations run wild.

With the birth of ready to wear, clothing manufacturers were able to slash costs whilst offering unprecedented choice. For the burgeoning middle classes, many of whom had made their money in the textile industry, the impact was huge: with a seemingly endless variety of textiles, available, women could show off their family

THE LUDDITES
Not everyone embraced the new industrial landscape

Though mill owners celebrated each industrial development that would bring about faster production and, subsequently, more money, not everybody shared their delight at the changing world ushered in by the Industrial Revolution.

In 1811, a gang of masked textile workers and weavers led an attack in which 1,000 brand-new machines were smashed across Nottingham and Derbyshire, beginning a spate of similar nighttime raids that would last for years and go through Leicestershire, Lancashire and Yorkshire too. These protestors were known as the Luddites and they wanted to show their dissatisfaction of the way in which machines had been brought in to do the work of humans, as well as their distaste at the way the human workers were treated.

The Luddites were a highly organised group who supported their machine-breaking activities with public demonstrations and letter-writing campaigns. Mill and factory bosses responded to their attacks by shooting protestors. The government's response was to call in the army to suppress the uprising and, following the shooting of mill owner, William Horsfall of Huddersfield, held a mass trial of Luddites at York in January 1813.

Over 60 men were charged with various crimes, though half of the defendants were acquitted. Those who were found guilty faced punishments ranging from transportation to execution and the government made "machine breaking" a crime punishable by death. With the stakes so high, the Luddite movement slowly faded, just as the government had hoped it would.

THE DEPARTMENT STORE

Fashionistas needed somewhere to buy their ready-to-wear garments; department stores were happy to oblige

....

The UK's first department store, Harding, Howell & Co, opened in 1796 in London's Pall Mall. It sold furs and fans, haberdashery, jewellery, and hats. Though it was the first, it certainly wouldn't be the last and the Industrial Revolution created a world in which the department store could flourish.

With the new mass-production methods, manufacturers began to produce ready-to-wear garments, offering a huge selection of clothing and accessories to customers across the social classes. Whereas consumers had once visited dressmakers and tailors where their garments would be created from scratch, now those garments were mass-produced. All consumers had to do was buy them.

Department stores sprang up in which shoppers could buy not just a dress or a suit, but a lifestyle. In these temples to consumerism, one could buy anything, but one could also find entertainment, demonstrations and other events to keep shoppers occupied and spending both time and money. Often grand, even palatial, department stores could be the jewel in the crown of a town or city, offering a glimpse of a lifestyle that seemed, for the first time, achievable.

Women in particular now had freedom to browse and the emerging middle class embraced the department store. With displays and ranges geared specifically to female tastes, the stores seemed to speak directly to women, who increasingly were making decisions not just about their own wardrobe, but about the homes in which they lived. For the first time, women felt as though they were the customer, not just his wife.

Department stores such as Harding, Howell & Co. offered women a place to browse and purchase

The mills and factories could offer work for all the family; however, it was gruelling and dangerous

wealth by stuffing their wardrobes to bursting. Though fashion had traditionally been dictated by the upper classes, in the brave new world of the Industrial Revolution, the tastemakers were no longer old money. Meanwhile, for consumers who had less money to throw around, there was still a far greater choice than before, which meant that the old traditions of adapting the dresses of generations past died out. For the poor, of course, all of this was moot: whether handmade or mass-manufactured, there was little chance that they would be able to buy a new frock for every special occasion.

But sewing machines didn't only play an industrial role, they were soon popular domestic items too. Now women who lived on a budget could purchase textiles or reuse old garments to make their own gowns, whilst even members of the working class could finally enhance their

> *"The old traditions of adapting the dresses of generations past died out"*

own wardrobes as much as their means allowed. Unlike hand stitching, using a sewing machine saved a vast amount of time, and for the first time fashion really was within the reach of the masses. A sewing machine was not an extravagance, but an investment for the household: it would make repairs and repurposing that much quicker and

Fashion and the Industrial Revolution

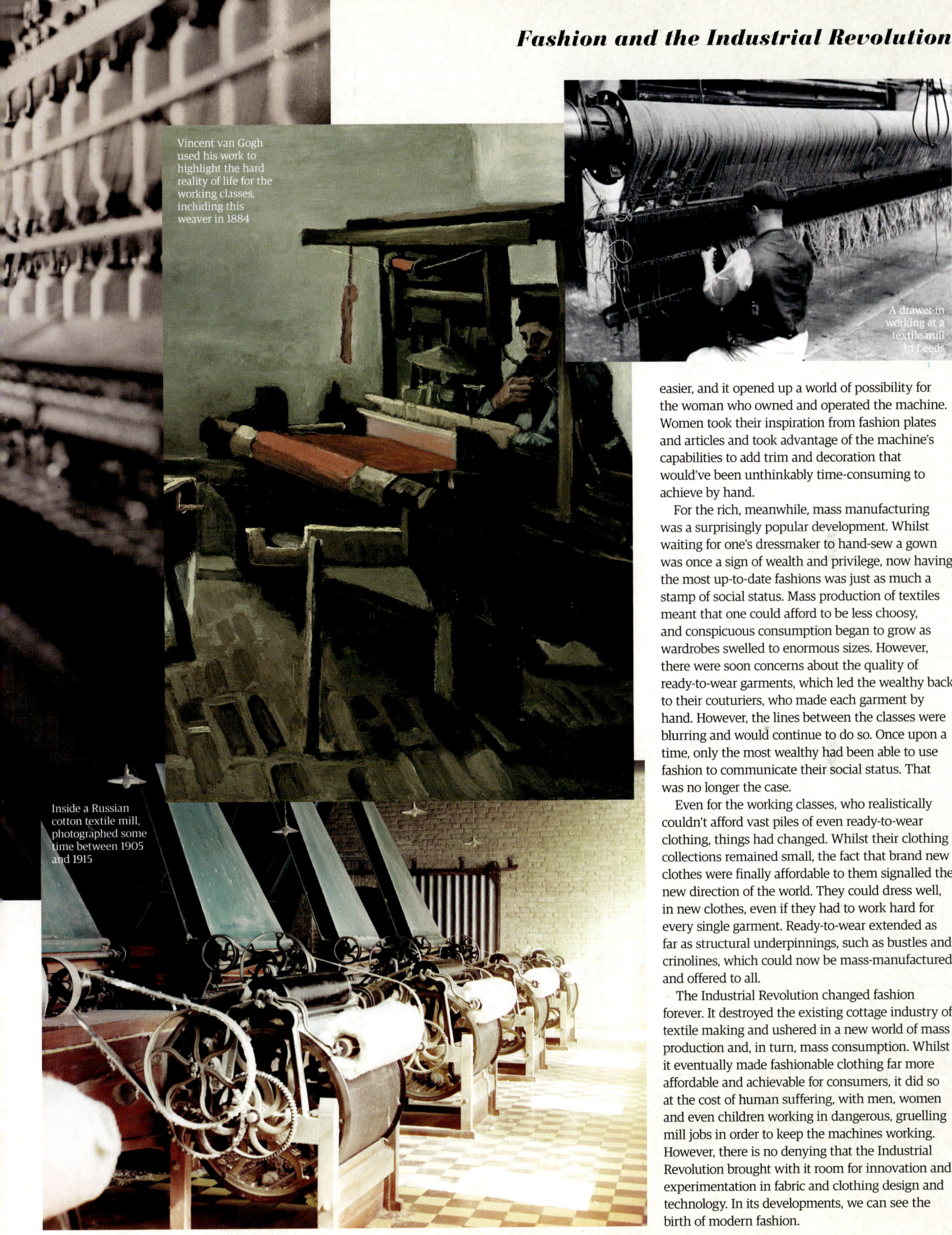

Vincent van Gogh used his work to highlight the hard reality of life for the working classes, including this weaver in 1884

A drawer-in working at a textile mill in Leeds

Inside a Russian cotton textile mill, photographed some time between 1905 and 1915

easier, and it opened up a world of possibility for the woman who owned and operated the machine. Women took their inspiration from fashion plates and articles and took advantage of the machine's capabilities to add trim and decoration that would've been unthinkably time-consuming to achieve by hand.

For the rich, meanwhile, mass manufacturing was a surprisingly popular development. Whilst waiting for one's dressmaker to hand-sew a gown was once a sign of wealth and privilege, now having the most up-to-date fashions was just as much a stamp of social status. Mass production of textiles meant that one could afford to be less choosy, and conspicuous consumption began to grow as wardrobes swelled to enormous sizes. However, there were soon concerns about the quality of ready-to-wear garments, which led the wealthy back to their couturiers, who made each garment by hand. However, the lines between the classes were blurring and would continue to do so. Once upon a time, only the most wealthy had been able to use fashion to communicate their social status. That was no longer the case.

Even for the working classes, who realistically couldn't afford vast piles of even ready-to-wear clothing, things had changed. Whilst their clothing collections remained small, the fact that brand new clothes were finally affordable to them signalled the new direction of the world. They could dress well, in new clothes, even if they had to work hard for every single garment. Ready-to-wear extended as far as structural underpinnings, such as bustles and crinolines, which could now be mass-manufactured and offered to all.

The Industrial Revolution changed fashion forever. It destroyed the existing cottage industry of textile making and ushered in a new world of mass production and, in turn, mass consumption. Whilst it eventually made fashionable clothing far more affordable and achievable for consumers, it did so at the cost of human suffering, with men, women and even children working in dangerous, gruelling mill jobs in order to keep the machines working. However, there is no denying that the Industrial Revolution brought with it room for innovation and experimentation in fabric and clothing design and technology. In its developments, we can see the birth of modern fashion.

63

SPINNING JENNY

Inside the mechanism that revolutionised fashion

James Hargreaves may have been an illiterate weaver but he proved himself to be one of the great inventors of his generation. His spinning jenny, which was invented in 1764 and patented in 1770, replaced the traditional spinning wheel that had been used for centuries and paved the way for the Industrial Revolution.

Laboriously operated by hand in people's homes, spinning wheels had long been the backbone of a flourishing 'cottage industry' in northern England but they could only spin one thread of cotton at a time.

Cloth merchants would provide the necessary raw cotton and pay a piecework rate to have it turned into cloth. The spinning jenny, however, allowed workers to operate eight or more spools at once, boosting productivity.

It was not long before merchants established 'jenny shops' and 'manufactories' where they could spin wool en masse. However, the machine was not universally popular. As the spinning jenny kept up with the textile industry's demands, the price of yarn fell, forcing weavers to accept lower wages. Hargreaves was forced to flee to Nottingham in 1768 as angry workers broke into his home and destroyed his machines. But the era of domestic spinning was over.

Even so, the spinning jenny did not last. While the machine led to greater scaling, its underlying process was the same as the traditional spinning wheel, relying on skilled labour to operate it, while only producing a weak, coarse thread.

Richard Arkwright not only refined the process so it produced stronger thread, but he hit upon the idea of powering the device with a water wheel. From this one central source of power, he could drive a whole network of machines.

While this meant he employed nearly 600 people Nottingham and Cromford in the 1770s, they didn't require the same technical ability, so he could pay them significantly less. The water frame was then replaced by Samuel Crompton's spinning mule and, in turn, the power loom as a new era of mechanisation dawned.

GUIDING THE COTTON
In order to guide the threads in to the right place on the spindle, it was necessary to have a pressing faller wire. This was released with a hand lever once the spinning was complete, bringing the faller down on to the threads. A counter balance tightened the cords.

VERTICAL SPINDLES
Before James Hargreaves created his invention, spindles on spinning machines had always been placed horizontally. Hargreaves, however, is said to have seen a small spinning wheel knocked on to its side and continue to work. He realised that the spindles on such contraptions could be placed vertically in a row, making it possible to draw and twist on many spindles at the same time.

LENGTHENING THREADS
With the thread extended and stationary, spinning the wheel ensured a twisting motion which would rotate the spindles and spin the thread into yarn. This would continue until the desired fineness was attained. If they were producing yarn that was intended to go across the length of a fabric (a warp), then it needed to be stronger than that going across the width (a weft).

LARGE MACHINES
Initially the machines were small enough to be used within people's homes but as time went on they became larger so factories were created to accommodate them. The cottage industry had thereby given way to the Industrial Revolution and, as well as refining and advancing the process of cotton spinning, profit margins shot up as a result.

THE ROVE
A rack of spools situated about half way along the machine contained roving – long and narrow bundles of fibre, or unspun cotton. One end of each roving passed between two clasping horizontal bars of wood before being extended and attached to an opposite spindle. The fundamental idea was that the thread would be spun from the rovings to the spindles.

Spinning jenny

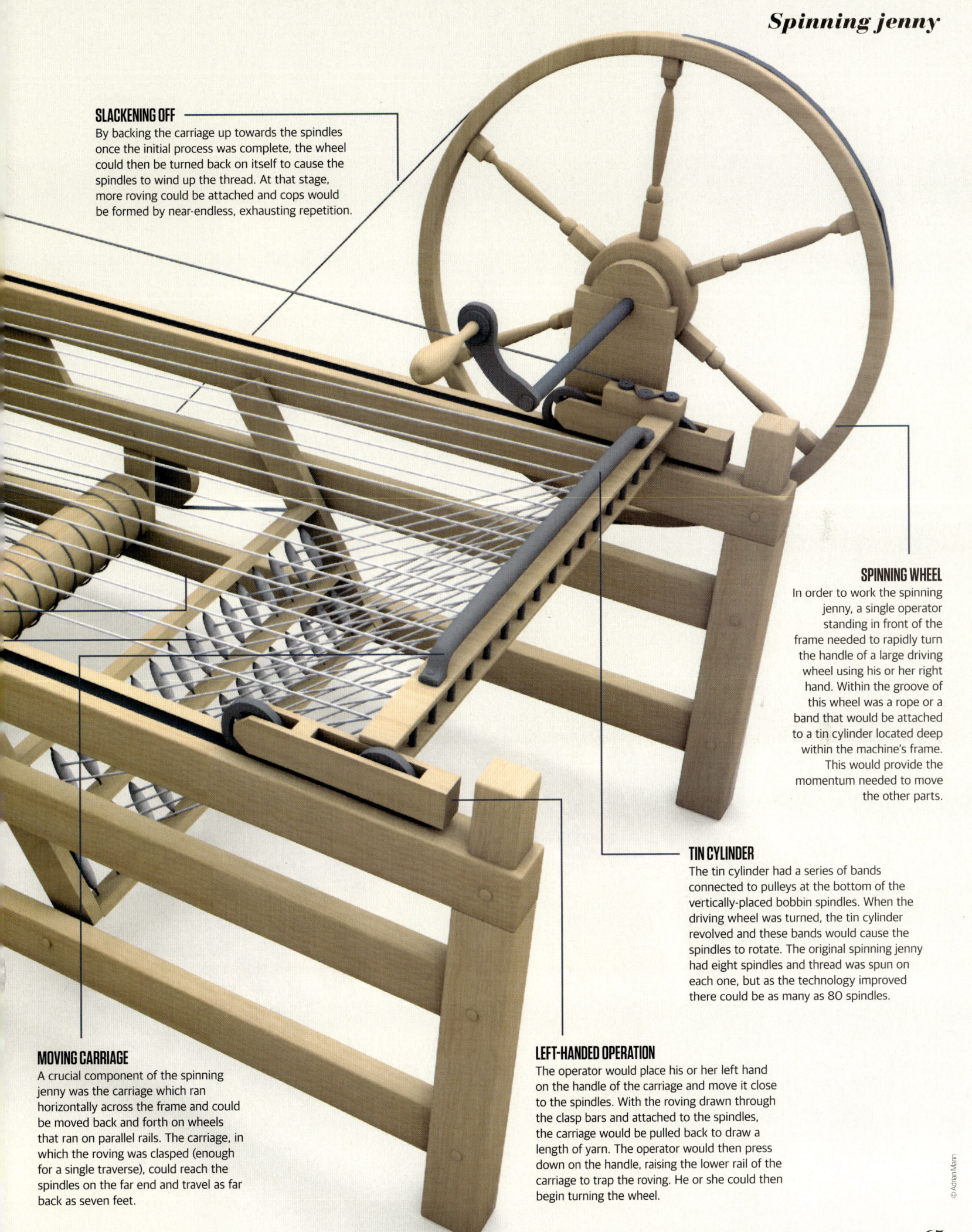

SLACKENING OFF
By backing the carriage up towards the spindles once the initial process was complete, the wheel could then be turned back on itself to cause the spindles to wind up the thread. At that stage, more roving could be attached and cops would be formed by near-endless, exhausting repetition.

SPINNING WHEEL
In order to work the spinning jenny, a single operator standing in front of the frame needed to rapidly turn the handle of a large driving wheel using his or her right hand. Within the groove of this wheel was a rope or a band that would be attached to a tin cylinder located deep within the machine's frame. This would provide the momentum needed to move the other parts.

TIN CYLINDER
The tin cylinder had a series of bands connected to pulleys at the bottom of the vertically-placed bobbin spindles. When the driving wheel was turned, the tin cylinder revolved and these bands would cause the spindles to rotate. The original spinning jenny had eight spindles and thread was spun on each one, but as the technology improved there could be as many as 80 spindles.

MOVING CARRIAGE
A crucial component of the spinning jenny was the carriage which ran horizontally across the frame and could be moved back and forth on wheels that ran on parallel rails. The carriage, in which the roving was clasped (enough for a single traverse), could reach the spindles on the far end and travel as far back as seven feet.

LEFT-HANDED OPERATION
The operator would place his or her left hand on the handle of the carriage and move it close to the spindles. With the roving drawn through the clasp bars and attached to the spindles, the carriage would be pulled back to draw a length of yarn. The operator would then press down on the handle, raising the lower rail of the carriage to trap the roving. He or she could then begin turning the wheel.

© Adrian Mann

DEMURE LADIES

The real-life fashions of the Regency period

Written by Emily Staniforth

Dresses of this era tended to be more muted and pastel in colour

Demure ladies

The fashion of the Regency era has captured the imaginations of many people, mainly due to the success of the beloved author Jane Austen and the many screen adaptations of her famous novels. It is not hard to picture characters like Lizzie Bennet wearing her bonnet and dress and taking her daily stroll. But how close are these outfits we are familiar with to the real-life attire of Regency women? At the dawn of the Regency period, which is generally accepted by historians to have been circa 1795 (although it is officially named after the later period when George, Prince of Wales was regent for his father King George III), a fresh style was emerging amongst the women of Europe. A new style for a new era, the Regency fashions were concentrated on differing from what had come immediately before whilst still taking inspiration from the ancient past. Neoclassicism was a huge influence on not just the architecture and decor of this era but its fashion too. Though women's fashions changed throughout the era, which is considered to have ended in the mid-1830s, much stayed the same in terms of the basic styles that remained popular. The lines, colours and styles of women's gowns during this period have a distinctive look that is immediately recognisable.

EVERYDAY DRESSING

After the voluminous fashionable skirts of the previous centuries, the 19th century saw a huge change for women. Women's clothes became more muted in every aspect. Everything became smaller and more refined: dresses, headwear, accessories, all could be described as understated after the extravagance that had come before. Skirts remained loose fitting, but instead of being expanded using undergowns and structured base layers, material draped downwards skimming the body to create a new fashionable silhouette. This shape is now known as the 'empire line', but dresses that were designed to this silhouette were actually not named this until the 20th century.

Empire dresses first became fashionable in France where, after the Revolution (1789-1799), people were looking to dress as differently as possible to the opulent and exaggerated style of the 18th-century French aristocrats. As a result, the empire style of dress developed in contrast to the enormous skirts from before. These dresses were fitted above the waist, retaining the low neckline that was fashionable in the previous century but adapting it to make the cut less wide and obvious. Everything about the empire dress was softer and more delicate. The material of the dress was cinched under the bodice-covered bust, giving the illusion of a high waist and long legs. The bottom of the garment flowed downwards and grazed the floor. This elegant new style was soon adopted by women across Europe who not only took their

ACCESSORISING AN OUTFIT
What else did Regency women wear?

1 SHAWLS

As dresses tended to be made out of thinner, flowing materials, it was important for women to accessorise in order to stay warm. Shawls were a hugely popular way of adding an extra layer of warmth and comfort to an outfit, and became a fashion staple. They could also be worn as part of a more elaborate ensemble in the evening, with some shawls made from silk or tulle.

2 JEWELLERY

Influenced by simplicity of the empire style gowns of the time, jewellery worn by women of this period tended to be understated and complementary rather than large and flashy. Gemstones like pearls, diamonds, topaz and amethysts were popular choices and pieces often featured designs inspired by nature. French Empress Joséphine's taste in minimal and less conspicuous jewellery helped to influence this wider trend of understated jewel accessories

3 BONNETS

Unlike the tall, extravagantly curled hair of the early 18th century, women's hairstyles during the Regency period were much more discreet and simple. From the 1820s, many women wore their hair under a bonnet or a cap during the day just as older women had been doing since the beginning of the era. Leghorn hats, which had a wide brimmed front, also became popular. Larger hats became more fashionable throughout the period, and as time progressed they became bigger and more ostentatiously decorated with feathers and ribbons.

4 OTHER ACCESSORIES

Women during this era accessorised with a number of other accoutrements, many of which had a practical purpose as well as serving as a stylish addition to an outfit. Beautiful fans helped to keep a woman cool, while parasols protected them from the sun while in the great outdoors. Hand muffs kept a woman warm and, owing to the fact that Regency gowns did not incorporate pockets into their designs, some women also carried small handbags known as reticules which could be worn around the wrist.

In this illustration, a Regency era woman is pictured holding a parasol and wearing a leghorn hat

inspiration from the new French trends, but also from the classical worlds of ancient Greece and Rome. A renewed interest in these ancient societies saw women wanting to replicate the fashions they saw in art and sculpture, and the empire style closely resembled the flowing togas of the Romans and Greeks.

Ironically, given the empire dresses' roots in ancient inspirations and the aftermath of rebellion, it was a fashion icon of pre-Revolution France who wore one of the first examples of this new style. The last Queen of France, Marie Antoinette, who had lost her head to the guillotine after the abolition of the monarchy and had been a symbol of the ostentation of the French court so despised by the revolutionaries, had attempted to endear herself to her public by appearing in a painting wearing a chemise à la reine dress. This particular dress is considered to be a precursor to the empire style. At the time, she was mocked for trying to appear to be one of the people and some even thought she

Demure ladies

The simple empire dress could be enhanced with a number of accessories

Empress Joséphine, a fashion icon of the Regency period, is painted here wearing a typical empire style dress with decorated sleeves

A simple evening dress of the time, featuring muted embroidery

> "The empire style closely resembled the flowing togas of the Romans and ancient Greeks"

was trying to make fun of the plainer fashions of the working classes. But, just a few years after her death, the most stylish women of the new French Republic were dressing just like her.

COLOURS AND MATERIALS
Once again rejecting the trends of the last centuries, European women in the 19th century turned to a more pastel colour scheme when dressing themselves for day-to-day life. Gone were the days of deep reds and golds and purples, and instead whites, blues, lilacs, greens and pinks became all the rage. Dyes were expensive and so many of these colours were pale in tone. The dyes of the time were not as vibrant as the aniline dyes that were discovered in the Victorian era, and so many Regency dresses were coloured using natural dyes, the vibrancy of which faded as time wore on.

Towards the end of the 18th century, when the new French fashions were starting to take hold across the rest of Europe, women's dresses were made out of materials like cotton and wool. However, as styles developed, more delicate fabrics began to be used. Silk and more translucent cottons like muslin allowed women to emulate the classical fashions they aspired to, and created a more subtle and light appearance.

SILHOUETTES, STAYS AND STYLES
To help create the desired empire silhouette, Regency women commonly relied on shapewear.

Famous Regency period author Jane Austen is pictured here wearing an empire style gown with an unusual high neckline and a bonnet

Like a corset, a stay would have helped to shape a woman's body into the fashionable shape of the day, but instead of minimising the waist it pushed the bust up to draw attention to a woman's chest: for women of the Regency period the more busty a dress was, the better. The stay came in two forms depending on what a woman wanted to achieve or on her body type. Short stays only went slightly below the breasts and were used primarily to accentuate the bust. Long stays, on the other hand, were worn by women who perhaps needed extra support in the chest area, or who wanted to smooth down their curves and appear slimmer in their delicate dresses.

Regency dresses, though more plain and simple than the fashion that had come before, were still ornately decorated. Embroidery was the main way in which garments were adorned, sometimes in a Grecian style. However, some women drew inspiration from military uniforms and trimmed their dresses with velvet or braiding. Others looked to fashion icons of the time, the most prominent of which was Emperor Napoleon Bonaparte's wife Joséphine. The Empress's love for silk dresses saw many women more inclined to turn to the soft and luxurious fabric. She was also partial to ribbon and lace trimmings, which then became a popular form of decoration. Gifts from her husband's trips to Egypt allowed Joséphine to adorn her dresses with eastern patterns which served as further inspiration to the women who admired her style.

Stays were an integral part of a woman's dress, and longer ones like these helped slim a woman's silhouette

Demure ladies

Evening attire worn for balls did not differ too much from a woman's everyday wear

"Regency dresses, though more simple than before, were still ornately decorated"

From around 1810, Regency dresses started to become even more elaborate in their design and decoration, though nothing like the dresses fashionable in the late Renaissance. Retaining the high waistlines, the upper bodice became more structured while skirts incorporated elements of lace, slashing, tiering and ruffles. It wasn't until around 1825 that the waistlines of dresses started to drop back downwards.

EVENING WEAR
During the Regency period, women in the higher ranks of society commonly wore different outfits for different activities, all of which differed slightly depending on their purpose. A dress for staying at home, for example, would be similar but ever so slightly different to a dress worn to go promenading in the afternoon. Popular overcoats, like spencers and pelisses, may also have been worn for outdoor activities in the day. Dresses worn during the day would have been simpler in style and more practical whereas in the evening a fancier garment would be chosen to wear to social occasions and engagements like balls, at which the fanciest dresses of all were worn. Unlike the muslin and cotton fabrics worn during the day, evening dresses were made from richer and thicker silks and satins. However, this was the most major difference between evening and daytime dress, with the styles for both purposes remaining fairly similar.

Empire style dresses remained en vogue, and trains attached to the backs of these dresses became a fashionable option for an evening dress. However, these outfits had to be suitable for dancing in and therefore would not have been too long or cumbersome. Longer, earlier dresses sometimes had to be pinned up to allow a woman to participate in ball dances without worrying about tripping. Between the late 1790s and the 1820s, elaborate decorative ball dresses went in and out of style, with lace, feather and velvet embellishments dropping in and out of fashion.

THE END OF REGENCY FASHION
Toward the end of the Regency era, European fashions saw a return of the larger skirt and an end to the straighter flowy dresses that had dominated early-19th-century style. For some, like England's Queen Charlotte, large dresses worn with hooped underskirts had never gone out of style, but for many they had to give up on their empire style dresses in order to keep up with ever changing fashions. By the time the Victorian era (1837-1901) was in full swing, the plainer, elegant Regency fashions were a distant memory and women's clothing was again centred around corseted tops and voluminous silhouettes. Women were once more taking up space and making a big statement.

"REGENCY WITH A TWIST"
How do Netflix's *Bridgerton* outfits compare to real Regency fashion?

The clothing of the Regency era is consistently seen on film and television, particularly in the adaptations of novels by Jane Austen such as *Pride and Prejudice* or *Emma*. But Regency fashion has become once more a topic of conversation in recent years due to the explosion in popularity of the *Bridgerton* series on Netflix. In the series, many of the female characters are dressed in the traditional and popular empire silhouettes that have become so synonymous with the Regency era, and the low necklines and accentuated busts featured on the show are also typical of the historical period.

The show's creator Chris Van Dusen is quoted as saying: "Everything is rooted in Regency times, but the volume is turned up... One example of that is that *Bridgerton* is a bonnet-free world. Our ladies wear hats, but they don't wear more traditional bonnets." The colours worn by the show's female characters are also much brighter than those that would probably have been worn in real life, with many colours chosen to reflect a character's personality.

Two female characters are pictured on the *Bridgerton* advertisement wearing brightly coloured empire style dresses

71

It was the uniform of the 10th Light Dragoons Regiment, the Prince's Own, that inspired Brummell

THE GREAT MASCULINE Renunciation

The story of Beau Brummell and the birth of the suit

Written by Mark Dolan

It is no secret today that in general, men's clothing is less colourful, exciting and, let's face it, fun than womenswear. Although for a good 400 years, men were decking themselves out in all kinds of fabrics, colours, shapes, frills, skirts and wigs, for the last two centuries it's been a parade of sharp lines, dark colours and flat silhouettes. The turning point in the development of menswear can be put in the ten years from 1789-1799, coinciding, not without reason, with the French Revolution.

In 1930, psychologist John Carl Flügel wrote that it was around this time that "man abandoned his claim to be considered beautiful", dubbing it "The Great Masculine Renunciation" and ascribing it directly to the political and social influence of the French Revolution. He succinctly summed up the shift, noting that while up to the end of the 18th century, wealthy and upper-class men had vied to be "elegantly or elaborately" dressed, as Europe entered the 1800s, these men strove only to be 'correctly' dressed. Men's clothing was no longer an arena for the display of wealth, taste and extravagance, but merely a way to avoid a faux pas.

It's worth noting, though, that Flügel, while making a reasonable (and highly influential) point, was one of the founders of the Men's Dress Reform Party (MDRP), an organisation dedicated to liberating men's aesthetics from their quietly formal hinterland in the interwar period, as well as an ardent Freudian. He may well have had ulterior motives in being quite so damning and unequivocal.

Regardless of Flügel's motives, he'd struck on a significant turning point in the development of men's fashion. The French Revolution bifurcated fashion along two axes: time, and gender. Firstly, gone were the frills, lace, colours, luxurious fabrics and intricate patterns of 18th-century men's clothing, and in were dark colours, simple fabrics – particularly wool – and plain, unadorned designs. Secondly, where previously both men and women were united in a love of bright colours, complex shapes and silhouettes, and intricate decoration, all this fashionable playfulness, all the creativity, all the expansiveness, was left solely to women, while men rejected such alleged frivolities in favour of the sober utilitarianism that embodied revolutionary ideals.

There is no single figure who more embodied these new fashionable ideals, and had more influence on menswear, than George Bryan 'Beau' Brummell. Although he was born in Downing Street to a father who was the Prime Minister's personal secretary, and so his tale is hardly a rags-to-riches story, he was not of aristocratic

BELOW Two centuries later, Beau Brummell's sartorial choices continue to shape men's fashion

The Great Masculine Renunciation

In the wake of the French Revolution, menswear took a decidedly more muted turn

stock. Given that almost all innovations in men's fashion up to this point had come from the very uppermost echelons of society, Brummell's rise remains remarkable. Educated, of course, at Eton, he was presented to the then-Prince Regent, latterly King George IV, and the pair became fast friends. This was to be a very significant relationship for the burgeoning dandy, as it gave him a path into society, where he would make his mark.

Brummell's signature look, which once established he never reneged on, centred around the rejection of the previous centuries' bright colours and elaborate, even ostentatious ornamentation, and towards fine details and exceptional tailoring within the confines of a colour palette of blue-black, white and buff, and fitted silhouettes that showed off the figure rather than augmenting or obscuring it. The product of Brummell's tastes, preferences, rejections of convention, and influences was the precursor to the modern suit, i.e. a plain white shirt, dark coat and full-length trousers, finished off with an intricately tied cravat.

It was Brummell's own particular life that really shaped his style; his pared-back colour palette, for instance, was taken almost directly from the colours of Eton College, where he first began to become interested in clothing. After Eton, Beau – at the time known instead as Buck – went on to follow the prescribed path and matriculated into Oriel College, Oxford. Although the freedom of undergraduate life appealed to Brummell, he was ultimately unsatisfied and left after only a few months to run off and join the army.

The regiment that Beau joined – the 10th Light Dragoons – was not just any old group of young soldiers. Back in 1783, Prince George had asked the King for a regiment of his own that he could lead – and dress – as he wished. His wish was granted with the foundation of the 10th Regiment of Light Dragoons. In 1793, when Britain went to war with revolutionary France, the Prince was officially made colonel-in-chief of the 10th Regiment, though it was made clear that he would not see direct service himself, and resultantly the 10th Regiment was largely ornamental, reserved for occasions where optics were of the highest regard.

The uniform Brummell was required to purchase for his life in the 10th included two garments that would become staples: a blue coat and white trousers. His later fashion choices would also often incorporate the kind of material used for the 10th's uniform, while his adherence to tight light-coloured trousers can be directly traced back to his time as one of the 'Prince's Own'.

During the early 19th century, when Beau was really starting to gain status as the most fashion-forward man in Europe, there was a general trend towards Neoclassicism that contributed significantly to his overall look. Since the middle of the 18th century, there had been a growing interest in the art and culture of ancient Greece and Rome, partly sparked by incredible discoveries at sites such as Pompeii and Herculaneum, and young men's experiences on the Grand Tour. Architecture began

DRESSING FOR THE WAR
The First World War gave a military feel to civilian clothes

A 1919 advert for Burberry's popular wartime garment, the trench coat

While it was the French Revolution that first overhauled men's fashion and brought about the beginning of the suit as we know it, it's not the only conflict to have produced a stark change in men's clothing. The First World War also had a major impact on how men dressed. One of the most significant aspects of civilian life during the First World War was doing one's part by tightening one's belt (figuratively!); spending less, using fewer materials, and doing anything to contribute to the war effort. Part of this was greatly reduced spending on clothes, and particularly tailoring. Mass-made clothing was cheaper and more readily available, leading to a much greater degree of off-the-shelf clothing rather than the bespoke one-off pieces worn by fashion leaders in the 19th century. This led to a general democratising of menswear and a preference for more casual wear and less formality in everyday clothing.

In addition to these trends, some particular garments arrived as direct outcomes of the war. Possibly the most notable is the trench coat, a garment that already existed at the outbreak of the war, but gained prominence – and its name – during it. Officers who could afford it began to buy long coats from Thomas Burberry, made of his new revolutionary fabric, gabardine. Unlike previous waterproof materials, which relied on ingredients such as rubber or wax, gabardine was light and breathable while remaining waterproof, which made it perfect for the miserable conditions of the trenches, albeit only affordable for those who spent comparatively little time in them.

75

NEOCLASSICISM AND FASHION

How fashionable young men took their lead from the ancient past

It is difficult to overstate the impact that ancient Greece and Rome had on 19th-century European design. The Neoclassical movement was sparked by the work of a few key individuals, such as James 'Athenian' Stuart and Johann Joachim Winckelmann. Stuart was an artist who travelled to Italy to improve his painting skills and ended up studying and adoring the works of ancient Greece and Rome. His book *Antiquities of Athens* (1762) was the first accurate work on classical Greek architecture and was hugely influential for architects and designers throughout Europe.

Winckelmann, an archaeologist and art historian, was similarly enamoured by the artistry of ancient Greece and Rome, and extolled the beauty and perfection of its paintings and sculptures in his seminal work, *Reflections on the Painting and Sculpture of the Greeks* in 1755. In particular, he singled out the Apollo Belvedere statue as a perfect example of the Greek mastery of form and the idealised male body. As interest in the ancient world grew, and new discoveries of ancient art were being unearthed, there flourished an appetite for visiting sites such as Rome, Pompeii and Athens (Lord Byron, on his Grand Tour, inscribed his name into the wall of the Temple of Poseidon at Sounion) and collecting ancient artefacts among the upper classes. Together, all of this fed into a fascination with the aesthetics of the classical civilisations, which played a major role in the ideals of men's fashion espoused by the likes of Beau Brummell, with his focus on form-fitting clothing and the simple elegance epitomised by Greek and Roman art.

Men's fashion became much more form-fitting and simple than the days of doublets and codpieces

The Great Masculine Renunciation

> "While the basic pieces of a suit remained consistent, the silhouette changed a little"

97 DOUBLE BREASTED SACK

BACK VIEW FROCKS

ABOVE The modern-day suit clearly evolved from the age of dandies

RIGHT The Prince Regent gave Beau Brummell a path into society, where he made his mark with fashion

to incorporate classical features such as columns and volutes, furniture and ornaments took inspiration from Greek shapes and motifs, and statues, such as the Apollo Belvedere and Venus de Milo, were taken to represent the ideal human bodies.

There are numerous references made by Brummell's contemporaries to his body, which naturally conformed to the proportions seen as representing the Greek ideal, and this physicality, combined with the fashion for Greek statuary and the overarching Neoclassicism of the period, allowed him to develop a style that utilised tight, form-fitting clothing that showed off and flattered his natural silhouette rather than obscuring it. The coats he wore were an extension of this; being the most sculptural garments in his outfit, they offered London's tailors the chance to create a shape that did not simply mould to the wearer but gave the impression of classical nudity through the use of well-cut fabric and clean, sharp lines.

The legwear that fashionable young men were wearing during the early decades of the 19th century would often be the tight full-length pantaloons favoured by Beau, and they would commonly be combined with a knee-high boot, with turned-down tops and occasionally tassels – one of the few remaining flourishes that harked back to the pre-Revolution days – which were equally as tight, flaunting men's calves and adding a military air to civilian dress.

Just as at previous points in menswear history, when the primary signals of power and sensuality were broad shoulders or a prominent codpiece, in this period the leg was the main event. Toned legs were in vogue, suitably on display in the dances being performed at society balls. The tight pantaloons and form-fitting boots of Brummell and his contemporaries were the perfect way to combine both the desire for the Neoclassical form and the necessity of flaunting one's shapely legs, while the light colours that were often worn (it was notably rare to have one's pantaloons match the coat) hinted at the heroic nudity of Greek and Roman statues.

While the basic pieces of a suit remained consistent towards the middle of the 19th century, the silhouette changed a little, with narrow waists and slightly broader chest and shoulders back in style, while trousers, with a slightly looser fit began to replace pantaloons as the go-to daytime legwear (you'd still don the pantaloons for a night on the town). The importance of shapely legs remained, though, and some men even resorted to padded stockings to fill out their skinny legs.

By the 1840s, the tailcoat, cut across the front at the waist but long in the back, was falling out of fashion as daywear, with the frock coat taking its place. This was a long, narrow coat, full-length all around instead of cut in front. It was also around this period that men began to match the colours of their coats to their trousers, in a style more familiar to modern eyes. The next major turning point in the history of the suit is the popularity of the sewing machine in the mid-1800s.

The sewing machine revolutionised tailoring as it slashed the time it took to produce men's clothing, and ready-to-wear garments became widely available. It was around this time, and through the next few decades that the suit really came to resemble the garment we know today: the lounge suit, with its shorter jacket and matching colours.

For the rest of the century, suits would remain fairly consistent, always comprising the building blocks of white shirt, waistcoat, coat and trousers, with small changes occurring as silhouettes fleshed out and narrowed, top hats fell to bowlers, and cravats vied with bowties for supremacy. Into the 20th century, suits continued to evolve in small ways, with trends and fashions altering their shape and drape as time went on. Throughout every iteration, though, the influence of Beau Brummell and the Great Masculine Renunciation can be seen, with straight, sharp lines, dark colours and the basic elements still holding strong, making men unrecognisable from those adorned in the bright, bold and frilly garments of the centuries before the French Revolution.

77

ICONIC STYLE

QUEEN VICTORIA'S WEDDING DRESS

There were many trends that were started during the reign of Queen Victoria, but the white wedding dress's popularity continues to soar to this day

The famous portrait of Victoria and Albert's marriage, by George Hayter, summed up the wave of romance that surrounded the wedding

Queen Victoria's wedding dress

A DARING DESIGN
Victoria's wedding dress was simpler and more daring than previous royal bridal gowns. Despite the chilly weather, the queen chose a low décolletage with bared shoulders. Victoria also emphasised her figure with a pointed waist on the bodice of her gown. William Dyce, head of the Government School of Design, helped create the pattern for the lace while the dress was created by Mary Bettans.

THE BRIDE WORE WHITE
Victoria caused a storm by choosing to marry in a creamy white gown, as coloured dresses with gold or silver embroidery were more popular at the time. The young queen, a keen follower of fashion, chose this partly to show off the lace, which was so important to her bridal look. The trend for white wedding gowns soon took off among the upper and middle classes, who wanted to show their own prestige by copying the queen, and the trend of white and cream dresses has endured to this day.

HONITON LACE AND SPITALFIELDS SILK
Queen Victoria wanted her dress to boost some of the cottage industries that were suffering an economic downturn. She chose silk satin woven in Spitalfields and lace from Devon. The Honiton lace was made to a special design that was destroyed afterwards so no one could copy it. Victoria's gown had a long flounce of lace across the bodice as well as smaller trimmings at the end of the half-length sleeves. The lace provided work for dozens of local women.

JEWELS FIT FOR A QUEEN
Albert presented his bride with a sapphire, diamond and gold brooch on the eve of their marriage and Victoria added it to her wedding outfit. The young queen described the gem, which featured a huge sapphire surrounded by 12 diamonds, as "really quite beautiful". It would become one of her favourite pieces. Victoria's wedding jewellery also included a necklace and earrings made from diamonds that had been given to her by the Sultan of Turkey soon after she became queen.

BRIDAL BLOOMS
Victoria shunned a crown for her wedding day, instead holding her veil in place with a wreath of orange blossom. The flower, which also trimmed her dress and train, signifies innocence and eternal love as well as being an ancient symbol of marriage and fertility. Myrtle, another traditional sign of love and marriage, also featured in the bridal blooms. For her wedding posy, Victoria chose a simple arrangement of her groom's favourite flowers, snowdrops.

SHOES, BY ROYAL APPOINTMENT
Victoria chose flat shoes for her wedding, produced by Gundry and Sons who supplied footwear for several members of the royal family from their famous shop in Soho. Made of white satin, the shoes featured a square toe and bands of ribbon crossing the foot in horizontal stripes. They were secured with more long ribbons that tied around Victoria's ankles.

THE BRIDE'S BELOVED VEIL
Victoria used Devon lace for her wedding veil, attached to her hair with flowers. It featured the same, special design used for the lace on her dress. It took local women in Honiton and Beer six weeks to make, providing much-needed work. The veil became one of Victoria's most prized possessions and she asked for it to be placed over her face for her burial.

A TROUBLESOME TRAIN
Victoria's bridal train was 18 feet long and was carried by her 12 bridesmaids. However, it was too short for them all to be able to hold it and walk comfortably. Instead, the girls ended up standing almost on top of one another and had to tiptoe down the aisle to stay upright.

© Illustration by Julia Lillo

79

The UGLY GIRL Papers

A series of magazine articles in 1870s America aimed to help women avoid ugliness, and achieve beauty – at whatever the cost

Written by Nell Darby

The Ugly Girl Papers

The 'Ugly Girl Papers' attempted to address Victorian women's concerns about their looks, hair, and build

81

Where could you read about how to colour your cheeks, get rid of spots, and emulate the glamour of South American ladies? In the 1870s, the answer was by reading the 'Ugly Girl Papers'.

The 'Ugly Girl Papers' were a series of articles originally published in *Harper's Bazaar* magazine, before becoming a book in 1874. The author gave their name simply as 'SDP'; these were the initials of professional writer Susan Dunning Power. The articles proved very popular with readers, who also submitted their own advice. Women of all ages sought to look as good as possible, and the 'Ugly Girl Papers' sought to enable them to do so.

However, the 'Ugly Girl Papers' were not just about physical attractiveness: as well as features on skin and hair, manners, movement and cleanliness were all covered. There were articles about physical health and the 'dangers' of being overweight, mental health, and the benefits of exercise and sleep. Self-confidence was also emphasised, with the Papers noting that "the first requisite in a woman toward pleasing others is that she should be pleased with herself". In other words, if a woman genuinely believed she was beautiful, others would believe she was too, regardless of how old she was. The Papers showed they were of their time, though, with some rather old-fashioned theories: for example, blondes were seen to be prone to freckles and spots, and were encouraged to take a dose of ammonia in water twice a day to help improve their skin.

Susan Dunning Power used her own experiences in the Papers. When highlighting how women should avoid putting on weight, she noted that she had suffered from anxiety several years earlier. She lost her appetite, spending her days working and walking. She would either omit breakfast, or just eat strawberries and "one Graham cracker". Other meals consisted of half an orange or some cherries. Whereas we would see her diet as disordered, she saw it as "resolute denial" - an example that other women should follow. Although she told her readers to never go hungry, she also saw losing weight as worth the effort. Power also encouraged women to eat salad, particularly lettuce, as it apparently contained opium "in its least injurious state" (Lettuce does in fact contain a calming chemical, but fortunately not that one!).

ABOVE
Women and girls have long grown up with a fear of being called 'ugly', fears which this Victorian cartoon plays on

BELOW
Ammonia was recommended in lots of the advice from the 'Ugly Girl Papers'

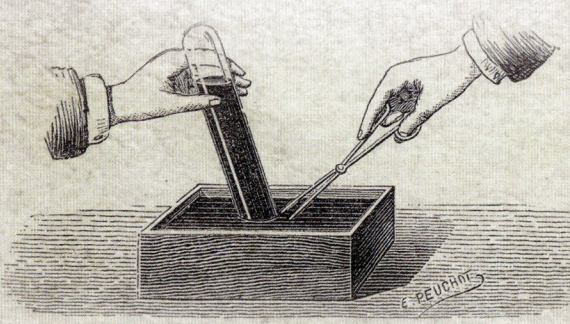

"The 'Ugly Girl Papers' considered ammonia to be one of the most valuable aids to women's beauty"

Although cosmetics could be bought by women, the 'Ugly Girl Papers' aimed to provide them with more natural alternatives

MAKING UP

In the 19th century, make-up was seen as unbecoming for decent young women, and was associated with prostitution and the lower classes. The 'Ugly Girl Papers' noted that artifice was commonly used to make oneself prettier - false hair and artificial shaped nails, painted eyelids and rouge on cheeks were "as old as Thebes" - but emphasised that it was only by using natural products that respectable women should attempted to beautify themselves. Paint and powder were a form of deception; using plants, for example, were not. The slapdash application of any make-up was also criticised, for it would "convey an unpleasant idea of dissipation."

More natural ways of making one's face more attractive could be quite hardcore; for example, one fashionable mother had made her daughter's lips redder and face more magnolia in colour by keeping her on a strict diet of brown bread and syrup. Another made her daughter's cheeks a

The Ugly Girl Papers

Spanish and South American women were seen to be the ideal of beauty

healthy colour by only feeding her oatmeal porridge. Both approaches were described in the 'Ugly Girl Papers' as being rather "courageous".

Other natural forms of hair care and make-up were recommended, with no mention of potential side effects. Hair dye to turn the hair black could be made from vinegar, lemon juice and "powdered litharge" (lead oxide). Shop-bought hair removers were seen as unpleasant because they were caustic and could leave the skin hard to the touch – yet moles, and the hairs that could grow out of them, should be removed with "lunar caustic" (silver nitrate). Eyelashes could be encouraged to grow by rubbing in lard mixed with mercury at night.

HAIRY REMEDIES
The 'Ugly Girl Papers' stressed that every girl should ideally have waist-length hair, kept in perfect condition. The hair should be trimmed once a month once and be washed daily or twice weekly with ammonia. Blonde hair was undesirable, and girls should be kept out of the sun in order for their hair to darken to "more agreeable shades". Alternatively, as blonde hair was seen as a sign of anaemia, it might darken if individuals ate lots of steak and red wine! Pomades were unacceptable as they were vulgar, and it was only permitted to oil hair if taking a sea bath, in which case, it would protect the hair from salt water – but should be washed off straight after, again with ammonia. The 'Ugly Girl Papers' viewed Spanish and South American women as having the perfect hair, long and thick, and twisted into a coil – in fact, in many ways, they were seen as the antithesis of the 'ugly girl'. The readers of the Papers were encouraged to copy their example by brushing their hair one hundred times a day.

DANGEROUS AND TIME CONSUMING
The 'Ugly Girl Papers' considered ammonia to be one of the most valuable aids to women's beauty. As well as the uses mentioned above, it was recommended that when a hot bath or a sea bath was not an option, women should use liquid ammonia in a pail of water for an invigorating bath, which would have the same effect as "a plunge in the surf". It could also be used for cleaning the skin, and as a deodorant by cleaning the armpits with a spoonful of ammonia in water every morning. No mention was made of the fact that it could irritate the skin or even burn the airways and lungs if accidentally ingested. Vinegar was likewise a common ingredient given for beauty treatments, and also recommended to bleach wigs to a lighter colour (although wigs were only seen as acceptable for actresses needing hair for theatre productions).

Chalk could be used to make face powder; it could be mixed with glycerin or wax from a tallow candle, although this latter was seen as old-fashioned. Such a powder was also recommended as it stopped women getting freckles – but breathing in such dust could have side effects such as headaches or lethargy. Although the 'Ugly Girl Papers' recommended avoiding rouge as it could contain lead or arsenic, its own alternative recipes were time consuming, if not downright odd. Face cleanser could be made from egg white, spread thickly on the face before going to bed, with a handkerchief laid on top to stop the mixture sliding off onto the bedsheets.

Although the 'Ugly Girl Papers' noted some of the dangerous remedies and products that had been used by women previously, it was not averse to recommending its own. Powdered saltpetre was recommended to remove freckles; carbolic acid could help with cuts and ulcers. Those who had been "exposed to low and degraded" people should apply diluted sulphurous acid (a strong preservative) – but if done incorrectly, it could destroy "all parasites, human beings or pets"! Luckily, the 'Ugly Girl Papers' did recommend avoiding using hydrochloric acid as a facewash, as one woman had done, as it could cause blisters.

The Papers were just part of a whole industry devoted to women's beauty by the late 19th century. There were pages of adverts in fashion magazines, and salons where one could receive beauty treatments. The 'Ugly Girl Papers' aimed to enable women to beautify themselves in the privacy of their own home, concocting their own remedies to improve themselves. Yet although they aimed to encourage women to make the most of their natural looks, the name of the papers, and some of the remedies suggested, also made clear that only some types of looks were acceptable.

MRS POWER AND THE POWER OF BEAUTY
The 'Ugly Girl Papers' were written by a young American mother

The 'Ugly Girl Papers' were written by Susan Dunning Power, who would later also write a children's guide to etiquette and good manners. Her magazine articles were just part of a long writing career.

At the time of her writing the 'Ugly Girl Papers', she was in her late 20s, and her only child, Andrew, was a toddler. The impact of motherhood and tiredness on her may well have got her thinking about how to look more awake, more youthful and more together, and to investigate methods of 'beautifying' not only herself but other women and girls in the United States as well.

Susan was born Susan Ann Dunning in Indiana, in 1845. Her father, Alva, a Presbyterian minister, was from New York State, and her mother, Ellen, from Boston. She was the eldest of several children. She grew up in Indiana and Wisconsin, and after marrying her husband Felipe, lived in a well-educated household where she was able to write for a variety of publications.

In fact, Susan was writing articles for the *Chicago Tribune* before she reached her teens. Later, she was on the staff of both the Chicago paper and the *New York Tribune*, and also wrote recipes for a Chicago womens' cookbook. Although she used her real initials on the publication of the 'Ugly Girl Papers' in *Harper's Bazaar*, she usually wrote as 'Shirley Dare'.

Susan, who was widowed by 1910, was badly burnt in a house fire in 1922, and tragically died of her injuries.

Susan Dunning Power wrote the 'Ugly Girl Papers' as a series for *Harper's Bazaar*; its popularity meant it soon became a book

83

THE TRIANGLE SHIRTWAIST FACTORY FIRE

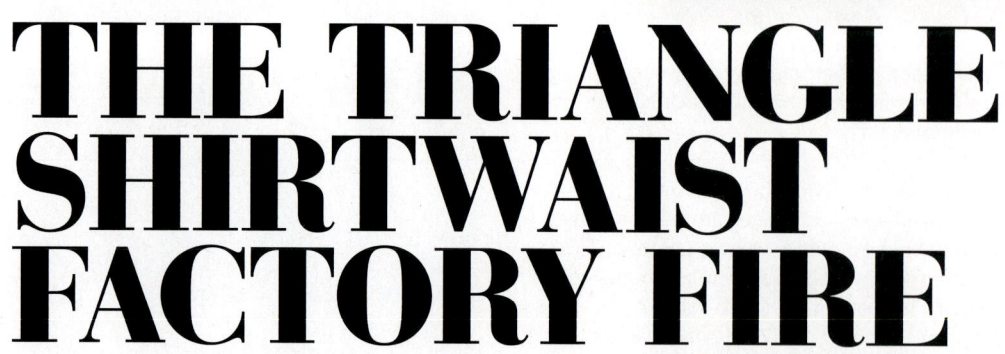

Inside the tragedy that paved the way for workers' safety

In the 1900s, New York City employed more than 30,000 workers in the garment-making industry. Most popular was the creation of the shirtwaist, a functional button-down blouse worn by many working class women. These were produced, most infamously, at the Triangle Shirtwaist factory. The women were exploited by subcontractors and bosses who cared little for the most basic workers' rights, and there was also little attention to the building's numerous fire hazards – it had already been ablaze twice in 1902. The fire on 25 March 1911, however, was by far the worst. While it led to new laws being introduced, it was too late for the 123 women and 23 men who perished.

STARTING WORK
Most of the 500 garment workers at the Triangle Shirtwaist Company factory were Italian and Jewish immigrant women aged between 15 and 23 and they worked on the eighth, ninth and tenth floors of the Asch Building in New York City. They were expected to be ready for their 12-hour days at 7am, if not earlier, for which they would receive between $7 and $12 each week.

CREATING GARMENTS
The work was relentless. The bosses would place a pile of material on one side of each worker's sewing machine and they had to get through the lot by the end of the day. For those on piecework wages, the faster they worked, the more money they would receive but all would toil in spaces so cramped that other workers would often have to walk sideways to get down the aisles.

TOILET BREAK
If the women became desperate for the toilet they had two options: to go during the one bathroom break they had each day or relieve themselves on the floor. The toilet was in a different building and, to stop the workers from sneaking out for a rest or stealing items, the owners locked the doors to the stairwells and exits.

The Triangle Shirtwaist factory fire

LUNCHTIME
Lunch had to be squeezed into half-an-hour but it was a welcome break, not only from the pedal work involved in operating the sewing machines but the barking bosses who would shout at them all day. Even so, the only daylight would be seen by those working on the front row of machines nearest to the windows. Gaslights lit the rest of the factory.

UNION ACTIVISM
Garment workers had already gone on strike over their conditions, back in 1909 when 20% of the Triangle workforce walked out. It prompted 20,000 workers at other factories to do the same but it was a struggle to get the Triangle bosses to agree to change and workers were denied union representation. Despite that, attempts to enlist others into the International Ladies' Garment Workers' Union continued.

FIRE! FIRE!
Beneath the large work benches on which the sewing machines sat were large waste bins that contained paper patterns and scraps of material. As people were thinking about leaving for the day on 25 March 1911, it is thought that a lit match was accidentally dropped into one of these bins on the eighth floor. A manager tried in vain to extinguish it using water pails while a bookkeeper sought to warn those on the upper floors. The fire took hold.

EVACUATION ATTEMPTS
A passerby spotted smoke billowing out of the windows as the fire engulfed the entire floor. He raised the alarm while the women inside sought to evacuate as quickly as possible. Some managed to get down the fire escape before it collapsed under the heat and their weight. Others tried the lifts but those who looked to get out through the stairway exit doors found them locked. Many burned alive.

DEATH TOLL
Firefighters hoped to rescue them but their ladders only reached the sixth floor. In desperation, many women – some in groups – leaped from the windows and died on impact with the ground. The lift had also buckled under the weight of those trying to escape and while some managed to get to the roof and move to other buildings, the fire claimed 146 lives.

Of the 146 who died, 58 had leaped from the burning building in desperation

Workers in garment factories operated in cramped, often sweltering, conditions for very long hours and with poor pay

The ROARING TWENTIES

As the world breathed again after war, fashion was undergoing its own revolution as it stepped out into the Jazz Age – Hemlines rose and stays were thrown aside, with bright young things ready to embrace freedom in the fashion-forward roaring twenties...

Written by Catherine Curzon

The roaring twenties

In the decades before World War I, the fashionable female silhouette was an unmistakable creation of impressive textile engineering. With narrow waists, long skirts and bosoms held in place by corsetry, women were shaped not by nature, but by strong foundation garments and structured clothing that didn't accentuate a woman's physique, but rather created and exaggerated the illusion of it, nipping in here and bringing out there. Often uncomfortable, completely impractical for women who wanted to do anything beyond the most simple tasks, and restrictive in many day-to-day activities, it was out of touch with the new world. Young women, caught up in the glamour and excitement of the dawning Jazz Age, rejected the concealing and confining layers that had been worn by their mothers and grandmothers in favour of something that screamed modernity.

> "This style offered its wearer a more androgynous body shape"

FLAPPER FASHION

Flapper fashion couldn't be more different from that of the generation that had gone before. Hemlines retreated from the ankle to the knee or, for the most fashionably daring, even above the knee. Those who considered themselves a little more demure still thought nothing of stepping out in dresses that flashed their hitherto concealed shins, now showcased by silky stockings. The accentuated silhouette that relied on petticoats and foundation garments was reshaped by upcoming design houses, who wanted to answer the call for a fresh simplicity with their own statement pieces.

In the 1920s, waists dropped lower and long, straight lines replaced curves and swerves. The 'la garçonne' look popularised by pioneers like Coco Chanel has become famous as the typical flapper dress, dropping in a boxy, straight shape from the shoulders to the knees. This style of dress offered its wearer a more androgynous body shape and revelled in simplicity rather than fussy opulence. When a fashionable woman wanted to dress up her look, she did so not with crinolines, bustles or layers and layers of gown, but with dazzling jewels and beads or glittering embroidery and sequins. The shapes were still simple, but feathers or bright ornamentation offered a shimmering evening pizazz.

For women on a limited budget, the new looks on offer opened up a whole world of possibility.

Flapper fashion was affordable, accessible and comfortable

With fashionable dresses no longer needing excessive yards of fabric and flapper looks easy to create with simple and affordable textiles, what had once been the purview of the rich now came within the grasp of the majority of women. Even jewellery became less extravagant; instead, a few statement pieces were encouraged and these could be as simple and sleek as the dresses they were intended to complement.

After centuries of wigs and ornamental hairstyles, flappers rejected anything that required hours spent in the hairdresser's chair. Their newly active lifestyles couldn't be compromised by hairdos that meant a girl couldn't move her head to the Charleston, and fussy hairdos were swept away along with the fussy clothes that had so recently been the fashion. Instead, women cut their hair into blunt, sleek bobs so they could wash and go, confident their look would survive all day and night. It was unlike anything that had been seen before and became an enduring symbol of the Jazz Age.

This Erté dress was the height of fashion, with its dropped waist and its Egyptian motifs reflecting the public's fascination with Ancient Egypt following the discovery of Tutankhamun's tomb in 1922

The roaring twenties

A FLAPPER
What did women of the 20s wear?

BOBBED HAIRCUT
Having recently won the right to vote in the United States, women in the 1920s were looking for ways to mark their independence and political liberty. A good example of this was the rejection of long-standing ideas of femininity that required long hair for women. The bob haircut was controversial at the time but a massive hit with the young generation finding their voice and style.

JEWELLERY
Inspired by minimalist artistic trends, the jewellery of the 1920s moved towards designs that were more Art Deco and simplistic. A great example of this is the iconic long-bead necklaces typical of the classic flapper look. These had the added benefit of moving around a lot when the flapper was dancing, a popular feature of their clothing, too.

MAKEUP
Advances in cosmetics combined with a desire for bold looks led to flappers wearing a lot more makeup, and more colourful makeup, than had previously been the case. With compact mirrors and metal containers for lipstick, being able to reapply makeup on the move was also easier. This made elaborate looks popular because they could be easily fixed or reapplied throughout the day or night.

STRAIGHT LINES
Continuing the theme of liberation, women were now free of something else thanks to this new fashion trend: corsets. The ideal of feminine curves was rejected in favour of a more rectangular silhouette that gave something of an androgynous look. Flapper dresses played into this with simple, straight lines. Where once underwear had accentuated curves, now it was trying to disguise them.

SMOKING
Part of the sexual liberation of women in this era included adopting behaviours that were deemed masculine, or at the very least 'unladylike', such as excessive drinking (all the more risky in the midst of Prohibition), swearing and smoking in public. Cigarette holders kept ash away from your dress and smoke a little further away from your eyes or hat. They also had the added benefit of drawing more attention to the act.

SHORT SKIRTS
Throughout the 1920s the hemline of the typical flapper dress began to rise, reaching to just below the knee, or higher, by the latter half of the decade. Showing off your legs was another scandalous act of rebellion on the part of flappers, rejecting the repressive views of women's bodies that had prevailed up to that point. Shorter skirts also combined well with the looser fit of the flapper style to allow for greater movement.

ECONOMY
The flapper style was not something that was only achievable by rich elites and the leisurely classes. While there could definitely be expensive variations on the style, dresses could be made relatively easily at home and the style of accessories was also relatively inexpensive. With the decade kicking off with an economic boom, this was a trend that any American woman could emulate.

Women rejected fussy hairstyles in favour of sleek, low-maintenance bobs

89

Dressed in Oxford bags, chaps about town were keen to show off their fashion sense

The roaring twenties

MEN ABOUT TOWN

For men, the fashion of the 1920s wasn't a dramatic change but it was no less welcome. Returning from the war, men who had existed in uniform wanted to show off their individuality once they were back. The slim, identical suits of generations past would no longer do.

In the 1920s, self-expression was encouraged when it came to male fashion. While slim fits could show off a sophisticated man's natural physique, not everyone wanted to be tailored to sleek perfection. Some men preferred wide-leg Oxford bags or plus fours when it came to trousers, while others embraced tweeds or pinstripes. Just as women wanted to express their individual personality through dress, clothing likewise offered a man the chance to show the world who he was.

Aiming to mimic the looks popularised by movie stars, men turned to a masculine silhouette, set off with starched white shirts and colourful cravats and bow ties.

In the 1920s, even footwear and outerwear became an expression of a man's character and social standing. For many, spectator shoes in black and white are symbolic of the decade, while for the real young male fashionista, nothing captured the 1920s like a raccoon coat. This fashion fad was hugely popular among male college students, who threw on long coats made of raccoon pelts and, accessorised with a pair of spectators and perhaps a straw boater, motored in their open-top cars from party to party. It was a look indelibly associated with youthful enthusiasm for life.

Both male and female clothes of the 1920s were looser and more comfortable

The affordability of 1920s fashion meant more men could own a suit

Women embraced the lower maintenance aesthetic

The roaring twenties

THE DEMOCRACY OF FASHION

In the 1920s, fashion became affordable for many who had previously found an up-to-date wardrobe to be beyond their means. Industrial production processes and less reliance on elaborate gowns and acres of fabric or underpinnings, meant that women could recreate fashionable styles from the most simple dresses. In addition, while exclusive design houses were setting trends for the wealthy, these trends were being copied and sold in huge numbers by department stores. Although only a few could afford a Chanel original, many more could afford the mass-market version. The fabrics used might not be so luxurious, but nobody would know that at a glance.

The same could be said for male clothes, too. With the boom in industry and manufacturing, tailored suits were no longer the exclusive preserve of the wealthy. Now a man with a far more humble bank balance could still enjoy tailoring that would give him Bertie Wooster's plus fours or Gatsby's sharp suits.

Even those who lived outside metropolitan centres could experience the new fashion frontiers. Department stores issued catalogues that were distributed across the US, offering even those in the most far-flung corners of the country the opportunity to buy fashionable clothing. For the first time in history, the contents of the richest wardrobes – or at least, an affordable version of them – was within the grasp of the working man and woman.

The revolution in fashion that occurred in the 1920s was truly groundbreaking. It wasn't just a development of what had gone before, but an entirely new and fresh approach. Things would never be the same again.

> *"It wasn't just a development of what had gone before, but an entirely new and fresh approach. Things would never be the same again"*

Chanel was out of reach for most people, but cheaper dupes became popular

ICONIC STYLE

EDWINA MOUNTBATTEN'S WEDDING DRESS

In keeping with the decade's latest sartorial style, Edwina Mountbatten's simple gown channelled flapper fashion

Edwina's bespoke dress was the height of 1920's glamour

Edwina Mountbatten's wedding dress

THE BRIDE WORE SILVER
George V's daughter, Princess Mary, had put her bridesmaids in silver at her 1922 wedding and now Edwina made it the star attraction. Her dazzling dress and its court train were made of silver tissue, specially woven for the gown.

ORANGE BLOSSOM TIARA
Edwina, like many royal brides, wore orange blossoms in her hair. They were formed into a high, crown-shaped headdress, securing her thin tulle veil. The flowers symbolise happiness and fertility.

FASHIONABLE FLOWERS
The bridal bouquet was a single stem of Lilium candidum, also known as the Madonna lily, symbolising purity and chastity. Edwina's bridesmaids carried delphiniums, which were also used to decorate the church.

TWENTIES STYLING
The dress had all the hallmarks of the early twenties with its simple silhouette. The dropped waist had stoles of silver tissue fabric falling from either side, covered in pearls and diamantes.

MODERN AND MODEST
The dress mixed high fashion and royal demands for discretion with its rounded neck, long sleeves with mitten-style cuffs and an ankle-length skirt, all finished with rolled hems.

PRICELESS LACE
Two pieces of Point de Venise lace ran down either side of the 1.2-metre train, which also featured antique Spanish lace. Both were gifts from Edwina's great-aunt Mrs Cassel.

HAUTE COUTURE
Fashion house Revillon created Edwina's gown. She also asked them to make her bridesmaids' dresses. Edwina's seven attendants wore on-trend delphinium blue with silver lace caps for their hair.

COURTING CONTROVERSY

The remarkable rise and dubious legacy of Coco Chanel

Written by Christopher Evans

Courting controversy

Chanel No. 5, the little black dress, the iconic interlocking monogram – these legendary hallmarks of the Chanel brand are instantly recognisable today, even to those with little interest in luxury fashion. Coco Chanel's classic innovations, which transformed the fashion industry and the way women look, have become indissoluble not only to haute couture but to mainstream pop culture and high-street fashion as well.

But who was Coco Chanel and how did she become so legendary, despite the controversies that still whirl around her past to this day?

Born Gabrielle Chanel in 1883 to a laundry woman and street vendor, the fashion icon's beginnings were notably humble as she grew up in abject poverty in the French countryside. At eleven years old, when her mother died, Chanel's father abandoned her and her siblings to an orphanage at a convent. It was here that she was reportedly taught how to sew clothing.

Her first work after she left the convent was as a seamstress, and at the same time she began

> *"The legendary hallmarks of the Chanel brand are instantly recognisable today"*

Despite her humble beginnings, Chanel's designs oozed luxury

The flagship Chanel store on Rue Cambon in Paris, which opened in 1915 and still exists today. This photograph was taken in 1936 when employees were on strike

singing in cafes and lounges. One of the songs in her repertoire was 'Ko Ko Ri Ko' and it is this tune that is attributed to giving her the nickname "Coco".

Whilst balancing a career in sewing by day and as a club singer by night, Chanel also spent time on the French social scene where she met a lot of wealthy men. At 23 she became the mistress to a textile heir and enjoyed a life of luxury living at his chateau, where he adorned her with diamonds and pearls. He also supplied her with the materials and resources she needed to become a milliner – designing and creating her own brand of women's hats.

Three years later, Chanel would begin an affair with one of her suitor's best friends – Arthur Capel, an English polo player and shipping merchant. It was with Capel's financial backing that Chanel was able to open her first store – Chanel Modes – in Paris, where she marketed and sold her hats.

Two more stores would follow and Chanel branched out into designing and making

Chanel's original 'Little Black Dress' from 1926

Coco Chanel in Vogue 1954

Chanel would watch her runway shows from a hidden spot above the salon

womenswear. In the 1910s, clothing for women was still mostly stiff and corseted, fastened together with buttons and lace, and altogether very time consuming. Inspired by the free flowing and casual design of menswear, Chanel began to create clothing using jersey. This material was deemed 'poor' and at the time was only really used to make men's underwear. The result was the Chanel jersey sweater, a simple piece of clothing that could be put on over the head, simplifying and modernising women's fashion in an instant.

Her revolutionary designs and unconventional use of such materials soon caught the eye of famous movie stars and the wealthy jet set. As her empire expanded with stores on the Rue Cambon in Paris, so did her success and by 1918 she was able to pay back Capel's investment in full.

Her ambitions didn't stop there. In 1921 the Chanel No. 5 perfume was born. The first fragrance to be named after a fashion house, the scent was

"Inspired by menswear Chanel began to create using jersey"

inspired by and designed to appeal to the liberated flapper subculture of women in the 1920s. It was a phenomenal financial and cultural success, putting Chanel firmly on the map around the world and becoming the lynchpin for her enormous wealth.

Next came the little black dress. Following the First World War, black was a common colour on the streets of France, reserved for mourning as widows grieved for the men who had not returned. This reportedly inspired Chanel to break tradition once again and use the colour for a simple and versatile garment that could be worn for practically any occasion, day or night. It became yet another huge success for Chanel, its straightforward design and mass appeal made it incredibly popular across the world and it even appeared in American *Vogue*.

The LBD, as it came to be known, became a staple contribution to the way Chanel's designs brought streamlined minimalism to the French fashion scene, which had previously been known for its pomp and opulence.

When France fell to Germany in 1940, Chanel was forced to close her fashion house. However, her wealth and social connections allowed her to continue living in the Ritz hotel in Paris, which had become headquarters for the Nazis. It was here that she met and fell in love with Baron Hans Günther von Dincklage, a high-ranking German officer. Although the level of her collaboration with the Nazis is disputed amongst biographers and war historians even today, it is well known she was anti-Semitic and involved with the Abwehr, the German intelligence branch.

Some have argued that her actions were out of self-preservation, but evidence suggests a more opportunistic motivation.

Courting controversy

For example when Jews were forced to hand over their businesses under the Aryanisation laws, Chanel attempted to use these anti-Semitic policies to her own advantage. When she created her perfume, Chanel had signed a contract with Jewish businessmen the Wertheimer brothers to produce and distribute Chanel No.5, and they would keep a majority of the profits. Chanel had long been unhappy with the business deal, which saw them make huge amounts of money off her invention, and saw the opportunity to ask the Nazis to return sole control of the business over to her.

Chanel's efforts were thwarted however, as it transpired that the Wertheimer brothers had fled to America and had given their shares to a businessman who wasn't Jewish and would therefore not be affected by the Nazi's laws.

In 1941 it is recorded that Chanel became Agent F-7124 and was sent by the Abwehr to Madrid. Under the codename "Westminster" – given due to her previous affair with the Duke of Westminster – and the guise of discussing business, she travelled to Spain where records show she met with a British diplomat. Little else is known of what Chanel did in Madrid, but shortly after she returned to France her imprisoned nephew was freed from a German detention camp, revealing the potential motivation behind her foray into political espionage.

Chanel would again embark on a mission for the Germans in 1943, when she attempted to smuggle a letter from the SS to her old friend, British Prime Minister Winston Churchill. The letter would advise Churchill that senior officers in the SS wanted to broker a peace deal, bypassing Hitler's authority. Chanel attempted to use an old high-society friend, Vera Lombardi, to get the letter to the British embassy. However, the plan imploded when Lombardi admitted her part in the plan to officials, whilst also denouncing Chanel as a German spy and forcing her to flee back to Paris.

When the war ended, Chanel was arrested by the French authorities and questioned over her role in

Although she never married, Chanel had a string of high-profile affairs including with the Duke of Westminster

Chanel had many friends in high places - including Winston Churchill

THE SMELL OF SUCCESS
The story behind the most famous perfume in the world

A 1927 ad for the perfume. The bottle design was rumoured to be inspired by whiskey decanters

Perfume for women in the late 1910s came in two forms – a simple floral scent for "respectable" ladies, and heavier musk for working class women and sex workers. When Coco Chanel decided she wanted to create her own fragrance, in her typical forward-thinking fashion, she wanted to capture something new and revolutionary, akin to the more liberated flapper woman that was emerging at the time. Envisioning a perfume that blended both the light florals with the stronger, less understated aromas, which appealed to all types of women, Chanel set to work. She recruited the famed perfumer Ernest Beaux, who had designed perfumes for the Russian royal family, and outlined her vision for a fresh fragrance that could last. Most fresh scents at the time were created using citrus notes, but these did not stay very long on the wearer.

Beaux worked for several months and presented Chanel with ten different samples. Out of them she chose number five and the rest, as they say, is history.

The secret behind the scent was aldehydes – a group of synthetic ingredients that added different smells to perfumes. Their distinct "soapy" smell helped create the "clean" scent Chanel was after, and their strength meant that they would last a long time.

Coupled with a unique, simple glass bottle design, standing out from more over-elaborate perfume containers at the time, No.5 was a runaway success, and became the financial lynchpin for Chanel's empire.

Still a major seller today, the perfume has been advertised by movie stars such as Nicole Kidman, Marilyn Monroe, and even Brad Pitt.

FORWARD FASHION

Four ways the fashion pioneer changed the face of women's wear

1 THE CHANEL BRETON SHIRT

The Breton stripe – a simple blue and white striped design – was originally adopted by the French navy as their uniform in 1858. It then became the seafaring look for fishermen and sailors, and in 1917 Chanel incorporated it into her nautical-themed collection and introduced it into popular fashion.

2 THE CHANEL 2.55 BAG

Named after the date of its creation (February 1955) the Chanel 2.55 handbag was, at the time, unlike any purse that had been seen before. With its unique quilted design, it was the first ladies' purse that came with a strap, so it could be worn over the shoulder.

3 THE CHANEL TWO-TONE SLINGBACKS

Designed to be worn comfortably day and night for any occasion, the two-tone slingback rebelled against women's footwear of the day. The two colours not only allowed the shoe to be worn with a variety of looks, but the beige slimmed and lengthened the wearer's foot, whilst the black tip shortened the end and disguised any wear and tear.

4 THE CHANEL PEARL NECKLACE

Chanel was a huge fan of pearls and used them in her jewellery along with other types of gems and stones. As real pearls were so rare and hugely expensive, women would be scared to wear them out on the street. Chanel was the first designer to incorporate faux pearls into her designs, providing a safer option for women who still wanted to look chic.

Model Paule de Mérindol wears a Chanel suit with slingbacks while posing outside the company's Paris shop

Courting controversy

Chanel photographed in 1954 in her now-iconic tweed suit. While her post-war designs were derided in her home country, American women aspired to wear a Chanel suit

Chanel models attend the funeral of Coco Chanel on 13 January 1971

A French document states, "A source in Madrid informed us that Madame Chanel was the mistress and agent of Baron Günther von Dincklage in 1942-1943"

assisting the Nazis. No charges were ever brought against her, and Chanel would later reveal this was due to intervention by Churchill. Once freed, Chanel fled to Switzerland.

Almost a decade later in 1954, at the age of 71, Chanel staged a return to the fashion world. Announcing that she was "dying of boredom", she set about designing a comeback collection. French fashion at this time had been changed by Christian Dior's New Look, a style which was almost the antithesis of Chanel's – elaborately ornate and heavily detailed clothing which included cinched waists and full skirts. The style was widely regarded as fashion's postwar renaissance and a rejection of the simple clothing of wartime austerity.

Rebelling against this, Chanel introduced what would become her iconic suit. Opting again for an unconventional material for the time, Chanel designed the collarless suit jacket and skirt in tweed, mixed with silk and wool, along with a trim and buttons that often contrasted from the main colour.

In France this comeback look was met with disinterest and derided for being old fashioned when compared with Dior's New Look. Across the pond in the US however, the suit was immensely popular and was even worn by First Lady Jackie Kennedy (famously on the day her husband President John F Kennedy was assassinated).

Chanel's comeback also saw the invention of the quilted purse with gold chain and her two-tone slingback shoes, both of which would become classic items in the Chanel brand (and beyond) and further cemented her legacy as an influential figure in fashion.

The changing face of the 1960s would see women revealing more of their bodies, and caused Chanel to remark, "I have dressed the whole world, and today it goes about naked!".

Since her death in 1971, the Chanel couture house has been headed by a number of designers, including Karl Lagerfeld who would update the famous Chanel suit and keep the label's designs up with the times through the 1980s.

Whilst the brand continues to be influential and in vogue to this day, Coco Chanel's personal legacy is still undeniably marked by her ties to the Nazis and her questionable actions during the war.

MAKE DO and MEND

In WWII, fashion was on the ration, but that didn't stop the ladies of Britain from finding ways to keep their wardrobe up to date, with a few pointers from the Ministry of Information

Written by Catherine Curzon

Make do and mend

Women came together at Make Do and Mend centres to share skills and exchange remodelled garments

Clothing ration books were immediately familiar to the people of Britain, even if they weren't particularly welcome

During wartime, the people of Great Britain faced deprivation in every area of life, with rationing introduced for many things that had previously been taken for granted. On 1 June 1941, new clothing was finally rationed too and would remain so until as late as 1949. Yet for a nation already used to making the best of things, this was just one more opportunity to show off a bit of imagination and ingenuity to keep clothes fresh and wardrobes up to date, even as the garments in them grew older and older.

The reason for clothing rationing was simple. With more and more civilians taking jobs in the military, suddenly uniforms were everywhere, and Britain's textile manufacturing industry turned its focus firmly towards war production. It was a matter of priorities: uniform took precedence over civilian clothing at a time of war. When the President of the Board of Trade, Oliver Lyttelton, announced clothes rationing, he took the country entirely by surprise, but the system that would be employed in this new arrangement would be entirely familiar to civilians. From now on, each item of clothing was assigned a value of points, according to the amount of materials and labour needed to produce it. These points were translated into the number of coupons needed to purchase an item, along with an amount of money, such as 11 coupons for a dress or eight for a man's shirt. Initially every adult was given an annual allocation of 66 coupons, but by 1946 this had shrunk down to a meagre 24 coupons. While children's clothes cost fewer coupons, growing children got through far more clothes, so they were allocated an additional ten coupons to make clothing them a little easier, while the Women's Voluntary Service (WVS) set up clothing exchanges to help mothers meet the needs of their growing children.

On 2 July 1941, the Board of Trade published 'Extension of the Life of Clothing - A Preliminary Investigation', which was aimed at providing civilians with techniques to make their clothing last longer. However, it was the Make Do and Mend campaign of 1942 that really captured the imagination of the nation. This collaborative scheme between the Board of Trade and a number of voluntary groups including the National Council of Social Services, the Women's Group on Public Welfare, and the Women's Institute (WI) was intended to educate people in dressmaking and

"Clothing rationing was a chance to show off a bit of imagination and ingenuity"

103

THE SIREN SUIT

A favourite of Winston Churchill, the siren suit was a must-have garment of WWII

In wartime Britain, the air raid sirens could sound at any time, so civilians looked for a garment that would provide cover and warmth if they had to run for the shelters. The clothing industry answered with the siren suit. Similar to a boiler suit, the siren suit was a one-piece garment that could be worn thrown on over everyday clothing in a matter of moments. It had breast pockets, pleats in the back and a belt; some, though not all, had hoods. It fastened with buttons or a zip and was made of a fabric that was readily available on the ration. Prime minister Winston Churchill was the man who popularised the siren suit, becoming an unlikely trendsetter in the process. He even had one in pinstripes, for those more formal occasions.

Though the suits were initially marketed as being easy to throw on in the event of a raid, when it came to selling siren suits or patterns to women to make them at home, the garment industry didn't focus on air raids, but fashion. Women were depicted wearing the suit not to run for shelter, but to pose and socialise. With accessories, victory rolls and a slick of lipstick, the siren suit became another way for a woman to express her individuality. Comfortable and practical, they could be dressed up or down as the wearer demanded.

Siren suits were popular with children for their practicality and warmth too, making them a truly universal garment. They really were the 'must-have' look of the war.

Winston Churchill was a devotee of his siren suits, becoming an unlikely trendsetter in the process

A shopper looks through a rack of women's Utility suits in London in 1942

Utility clothing didn't mean drab; these Norman Hartnell-designed pieces offered a designer experience at a fraction of the price

"It wasn't only women and housewives who were expected to learn"

tailoring, knitting, needlework, garment mending, care and storage. By proper utilisation of these skills, people would be able to make their own clothes from scratch, mend those that were damaged or adapt old garments into new; it was to prove invaluable. In a country that had been making do for a while already, the scheme was received with enthusiasm and people pitched in, ready as ever to do their bit.

In 1943, the Ministry of Information released a newsreel to support the Make Do and Mend campaign, offering advice on how to make the best of the current situation and learn new skills that would make life much easier. The focus was very much on the 'can do' approach of a nation that was pulling together. It wasn't a question of if one could learn the new skills required, but how one would implement them. It wasn't only women and housewives who were expected to learn either; everyone was encouraged to improve their skills.

The Board of Trade published a booklet in support of the scheme in 1943, offering practical suggestions, advice and easy-to-follow tips for the novice. In order to give the policy a friendly face, a character named Mrs Sew And Sew was introduced in booklets and on posters, soon becoming instantly recognisable as she offered hints and advice to her audience. This friendly little doll was a skilled dressmaker and mender and as well as her instructional leaflets and posters, she came to life via animation to encourage people to pick up a

Make do and mend

Second-hand clothes were restored and resold to help ease the clothes-rationing problem

needle and thread. Making clothes was cheaper and cost fewer coupons than buying ready-made garments and people soon began to find novel ways to expand their wardrobes.

Knitting became a hugely popular pastime, but even that took coupons to buy wool, so old blankets and holed sweaters were unravelled so their wool could be reused. Some canny customers brought up vast lengths of unrationed darning thread and used it to knit or crochet garments until the government got wise and started selling it in shorter lengths instead. From unrationed fabrics such as blackout curtains to old sheets and bedclothes, people used everything they had in pursuit of the make do and mend. For the wives and mothers of men who had gone off in uniform and left their wardrobes behind, meanwhile, there were rich pickings to be found as those abandoned male suits became smart jackets and skirts for the women of the house. Perhaps most famously of all, silk escape maps issued to Allied aircrew found a new life as lingerie, having been sold off by the government when no longer needed or even handed over as a romantic gift. Throughout the war parachute silk was highly sought after for lingerie, nightgowns and wedding dresses, though it was not easy to come by. With elastic in very short supply, women's knickers were one of a very limited number of civilian garments that allowed the use of elastic throughout the war.

Just as the country had pulled together since the start of the war, it did so in the era of Make Do and Mend too. The press enthusiastically supported the campaign, devoting acres of newsprint to practical guides on pattern cutting and dressmaking, as well as caring for and mending garments, not to mention seeing off moths. Meanwhile, those who had the will but not the skill could attend free evening classes taught by the WI and the WVS, where expertise could be exchanged and new techniques learned. Of course, these classes served another valuable purpose too, creating a social space for women to spend time outside of the home, while still doing their bit.

All of this may suggest that the people of Britain must have looked rather tatty during wartime, but nothing could be further from the truth. By learning new skills, sharing their expertise and employing

ABOVE
The Ministry of Information's Make Do and Mend pamphlet was a how-to guide for dealing with everything from a difficult darn to the "moth menace"

some old-fashioned ingenuity, those who embraced the spirit of make do and mend could mimic fashionable looks on a budget, using what they already had at home. But there were other options too, some of them offering a surprisingly designer experience at a bargain basement price.

From 1941 the 'Utility' clothing range came on the market, which was a government scheme to produce smart and wearable clothes using a very limited range of textiles. Though basic, they were

Utility clothing was instantly recognisable by its CC41 label, guaranteeing affordable quality

FEED SACK FASHION

Make do and mend wasn't the first time a little ingenuity was required when it came to wardrobes

When the Great Depression swept America, it brought with it utter devastation; even the simplest item became a luxury and for many, buying new dresses was unthinkable. With 'making do' becoming a national necessity, women began to use cotton flour and feed sacks to make clothes for themselves and their children. Once the flour manufacturers learned how their sacks were being utilised, they began to print brightly coloured patterns on the sacks, along with instructions for how to wash the sacks prior to turning them into garments. Even better, these instructions were printed using an ink that would wash out, while the patterns would not.

The national press got on board and published tips and tricks for using the sacks to their full potential and soon, they were everywhere. Virtually indistinguishable from regular fabrics, they offered families the chance to make their own clothing that was bright and colourful. In a time when life was gruelling, it was an important way of ensuring that people could maintain dignity and face the world looking put-together and confident.

The intricate, often beautiful or playful patterns remained in use until the war years, when cotton sacks were replaced by paper, as cotton was needed for the war effort. Yet for more than a decade these sacks became not only clothes, but bedsheets, curtains and other textiles too. Today they are on display in some of the greatest museums in the world, a testament to the skill, talent and ingenuity of the women of Depression-era America.

This dress was made by Dorothy Overall of Kansas and demonstrates how a humble feed sack could become a beautiful garment

"Women were able to wear clothes that reflected their personal tastes"

Clothing rationing was introduced in Great Britain in 1941 with shoppers using coupons to buy their essentials

well-made and attractive clothes which offered excellent value for money. The Utility label became even more attractive in 1942 when the Board of Trade partnered with the Incorporated Society of London Fashion Designers to commission designers including Norman Hartnell and Hardy Amies to design Utility items. Suddenly, one could buy designer looks on the ration. Offering great value for money and coupons, customers knew that any garment bearing the Utility label 'CC41' carried with it a guarantee of quality and value.

For women in the workplace, who weren't issued with overalls or uniform, make do and mend was an invaluable skill. They were able to create garments to wear in a professional setting from those that they or their men already owned. Alternatively, they could pick up one of the many Utility garments on offer, perhaps buying an Edward Molyneux-designed coat for 30 shillings (£1.10s), as opposed to the £30 it would have cost before the war. Individual style flourished and women were able to wear clothes that reflected their personal tastes and individuality, including homemade jewellery and accessories, to add some personal flare. Though looking too showy wasn't recommended, lest people thought someone was taking more than their share, looking put-together was encouraged. Standards were not supposed to slip just because there was a war on.

As the war progressed, restrictions grew ever tighter and in 1942 and 1943, the government issued the Making-up of the Civilian Clothing

Make do and mend

The Women's Voluntary Service set up clothing exchanges to help mothers clothe their growing children

With an increase in cycling during the war due to petrol rationing, women's fashion began to change

REINFORCE CHILDREN'S CLOTHES
They will last twice as long

LEFT
In the drive for the war effort, the women of Britain were encouraged to keep their children's clothes going for as long as possible

(Restrictions) Orders to further minimise costs and materials. Men saw their lapel sizes slashed and the double-breasted suit banned, with fashionable trouser turn-ups banned outright, leading some to dodge the ban by deliberately buying trousers that were too long and having them taken up by make do and menders, conveniently creating turn-ups in the process.

The era of make do and mend far outlasted the war and created a generation of women who carried with them a litany of garment creation and care skills. The legacy of the Utility scheme, which ended in 1952, was that of a public who now demanded quality at a good price, leading to new regulations in the garment industry. Though it was through necessity rather than choice or design, make do and mend led to a new culture of sustainability, a world away from the fast and disposable fashion of the 21st century. Most importantly of all, it showed just what the women of Great Britain could do with even the humblest ingredients and skills, creating smart, up-to-the-minute looks out of virtually nothing. There might well have a been a war on, but that wasn't going to stop the march of fashion.

DIOR'S NEW LOOK

How Christian Dior's extravagant designs put the frill back into post-war fashion

Written by Louise Quick

Dior's New Look in 1947 was led by the iconic Bar Suit, a wasp-waisted white jacket with a hip-padded full black skirt

Dior's New Look

Say 'Dior' and most people think of luxury, haute couture and leggy models strutting up and down the runway in the latest high-end fashions. But before becoming one of the world's biggest and most recognised fashion brands, it was just one man, Christian Dior, struggling to make his mark in war-torn Europe.

It was 12 February 1947 when the designer's scandalous 'New Look' shocked post-World War II society and revolutionised the fashion industry forever. Taking place just under two years after Victory in Europe Day, Dior stunned the world's fashion elite when he presented his debut collection in Paris. Models swanned past in swathes of rich fabric, long, heavy skirts and dresses cinched at the waist. The story goes that one influential onlooker, Carmel Snow, editor of *Harper's Bazaar*, was so shocked that she declared Dior's collection a truly "new look" — and the name stuck.

Dior's designs, made up of two fashion lines named En Huit and Carolle, were all about creating an overtly womanly hourglass silhouette. It was a figure that, for better or worse, set the standard for fashion and femininity for the next decade, reflected in the famous styles of 1950s Hollywood stars such as Marilyn Monroe.

Among the impressive 90 pieces that made up Dior's collection that day, the real headline act was the Bar Suit. Still heralded today, it summed up the New Look: a large, dark, corolla skirt, padded at the hips, teamed with a cream blazer that cinched in and kicked out from the waist.

Following rave reviews, the designs spread across Europe like wildfire and made their way over the Atlantic to New York City. Many praised Dior with having single-handedly revived Paris' struggling post-war fashion industry. His designs were most popular, of course, among society's glamorous upper class. Hollywood leading ladies Ava Gardner and Rita Hayworth were both said to be fans. However, his most prestigious fanbase actually came from within the British royal family — namely Princess Margaret.

The fashionable young royal was a huge fan — so much so that she chose one of Dior's designs for her 21st birthday. It was immortalised in a famous portrait by photographer Cecil Beaton in 1951. Perched on a sofa, straight-backed and stoic, her small frame sits atop swathes and swathes of luxurious fabric that make up her almost Disney princess-like gown.

While these designs may seem glamorous, they don't necessarily seem shocking or particularly fashion-forward today. To understand the hype, it's important to appreciate the huge effect that the war had had on everyday fashions.

During World War II, the fashion industry was hit not only by rationing and austerity measures but, with the war's hefty demand of fabric and labour, there was a significant reduction in raw materials, skilled workers and factory space. Ultimately, the fashion of the early 1940s was dominated by simple suits and knee-length dresses with boxy, almost militaristic shoulders.

With the introduction of rationing in Britain in 1941, simpler, slimmer outfits became more popular as more coupons were needed for more fabric and skilled handiwork. This was also the year that most silk was commandeered to make parachutes for the Royal Air Force. Adornments such as pleats, ruching, embroidery and even pockets were restricted under austerity measures while additions such as hats and lace — deemed luxury items — were heavily taxed.

After food, clothing was the hardest hit by the demands of the war effort, which explains the series of 'Make-Do And Mend' campaign posters and pamphlets issued by the government. What you wore became a direct reflection of your contribution to the war effort. A band of London designers even came together to form the Incorporated Society of London Fashion Designers (IncSoc), to popularise austerity-friendly designs.

In 1942, IncSoc created 32 designs of so-called 'utility styles' — fashionable outfits that used limited resources — that they then presented to the public. Restricted to tight fabric rations, the resulting coats, dresses and suits were said to have no pleats, tucks or frills with no 'unnecessary' buttons. They were intended for all seasons, with paper patterns made available for those wishing to make them at home.

Reactions were mixed. While many of the leading fashion houses and magazines were happy with the surprisingly sleek designs, other fashion-conscious

Dior poses with models after a fashion show at the Savoy Hotel, London in 1950

The New Look's skirt lengths were much longer than fabric rationing had previously allowed

> "It was actually the long skirts that seemed to cause the most controversy"

folk were unsure about the cookie-cutter styles. The *Daily Mail* argued, "Mrs 'Jones' is nervous that she will walk out to coffee one morning in a Mayfair-style suit and meet her neighbour in, if not the same colour, the identical cut." On the other hand, another critic thought these Mayfair designs were actually too fashion-oriented and "not sufficiently practicable for the housewife or the woman in the war factory".

Whatever their feelings, these simpler, utility-style designs became the general trend, representing both fashion and the home front's dedication to the war effort. For a large part of society, this was an attitude not only reserved for wartime, but something that carried on, and in some cases intensified, in the years following the conflict. In fact, clothes rationing ended in 1949, and food restrictions lingered until 1954.

It must have been shocking to see visions of Dior's models enveloped in layers of lavish materials, covered in fine details and accessories. While IncSoc's utility-style dresses were rigorously restricted and made sure to use no more than 1.8 metres of fabric, it is said that Dior's more elaborate

The utility-style dresses that were all the rage during World War II

UTILITY CLOTHING VERSUS THE NEW LOOK

LET'S GET CREATIVE
When resources were low, people used their imaginations. Some used aircrew's outdated escape maps to make blouses, scraps of factory plastic for jewellery, wedding dresses from parachutes, and beetroot juice as lipstick.

BRING A BAG
Pockets and buttons were both deemed an unnecessary expense. While never banned outright, coats were limited to three pockets maximum and buttons were restricted to only the necessary in 1942.

THE SQUARE SHOULDER
Practicality was key with suits and dresses of wartime Britain. Outfits had to be suitable for everyday use and all seasons. This often resulted in practical, military-style shoulders.

COAT FOR DAYS
Like skirts and dresses, coats got bigger and more luxurious. Women were taking up as much room as possible in voluminous, often shapeless, coats that used swathes of fabric.

ALWAYS MORE ACCESSORIES
Elegant hats, belts that synch the waist, glittering jewels, shawls that reach the ground, dainty gloves that reach your elbows, the odd crown. With accessories, one was never enough.

PLAINER THE BETTER
Embroidery and lace on clothing were banned under wartime austerity measures, as was fancy details on corsets and ruching on women's underwear. So wartime fashion tended to be plain with few embellishments.

KNEE-LENGTH SKIRTS
Wartime rationing and a demand on materials for uniforms meant there was less fabric for everyday clothing. So slimmer, shorter skirts and dresses that stopped at the knee became popular.

SOMETHING IN THE AIR
A drop of perfume was the finishing touch to any glamorous look. Dior allegedly sprinkled Miss Dior in the air before debuting his famous 'New Look' as a finishing touch.

BIG, LONG SKIRTS
The end of austerity meant the end of size considerations. Skirt hems dropped to mid-shin, which was seen as more elegant and extravagant, and were full of hip-accentuating pleating.

ALL IN THE DETAIL
Pleats, ruching, embroidery and lace were all back in fashion. Dresses had plenty of dainty floral designs, elegant ruching and capped sleeves that showed off feminine shoulders.

Dior's New Look

offerings often contained over 18 metres each. This unapologetically glamorous and feminine style was a complete rejection of the wartime austerity that had been gripping the entirety of Europe so tightly.

The world's fashionistas, for the most part, approved of the lavish designs and the move away from the stale trends of wartime. "The bulkiness of the coats and capes to go over these tremendous skirts is startling," said one reporter for *The New York Times*. "Wide sunray pleats each backed in taffeta and slashed open to the knee are so manipulated that the swing of the skirt is a gracious thing."

Covering the collection in 1948, another journalist, who was particularly taken by the pockets, wrote, "One felt that these were an integral part of the costume for it added great style to see the manikins thrust their hands into them, pushing them slightly forward in a gesture that contributed immeasurably to the movement of the full skirts."

Strangely, among the waspish waists, exaggerated bosoms and extravagant accessories, it was actually the long skirts that seemed to cause the most controversy. While 1940s fashion had generally seen skirts and dresses stop somewhere around the knee, the New Look wasn't concerned with fabric rationing and so its hems sat around the mid-shin instead. To some, those seemingly inconsequential inches were seen as a snub to the war effort itself.

Christian Dior fits one of his dresses to a model

Models wearing Dior's dresses in 1957

Barbara Goalen models a 1947 New Look evening dress

However, back in the 1940s, Dior and his family had seen their fair share of involvement in the war. Born in Normandy in 1905, his family moved to Paris when he was a child and the family name was best associated with his father's lucrative fertiliser company. As an adult, Dior was always submerged in the capital's creative scene, eventually falling under the guidance of Robert Piguet — the same fashion designer who is said to have trained Hubert de Givenchy. This was short-lived and, at 35 years old, Dior was called up for military service in 1940.

After his two-year service, he returned to the capital where he was scooped up as a designer by the prominent couturier Lucien Lelong. It is said that while Dior worked for Lelong, the team, like many fashion houses during the French Occupation, dressed the wives and family members of elite Nazis and French collaborators.

However, when Hitler tried to move Parisian haute couture to Berlin, Lelong travelled to Germany just to argue against it. He won that battle, saving a workforce of roughly 25,000 women, often seamstresses working in specialised fields of embroidery or beading, that was partly made up of Jewish refugees.

Meanwhile, Dior's sister Catherine was a member of the French Resistance. Allegedly part of the Polish intelligence unit based in France, she was eventually arrested and imprisoned in a concentration camp in 1944 until its liberation in 1945. Two years later — in the same year that he launched his famous 'New Look' — Dior released his first and most famous fragrance, Miss Dior, named after his sister.

By the time Dior made the cover of *Time* magazine in 1957, he was easily considered one of the world's most famous Parisians. However, just a few months later — and only one decade after he was first launched into the spotlight with his New Look — the designer died of a heart attack while on holiday in Italy at 52 years of age.

While it was a shock to everyone, Dior had already personally named his successor and the role of artistic director fell on the shoulders of a young assistant by the name of Yves Saint Laurent. However, he only managed to run the company for a few years as he was called back to his home country of Algeria for military service — but he did eventually begin his own self-titled label in 1962.

As a brand, Dior has launched countless perfumes as well as make-up and fashion collections over its 70-year history, each time pushing different trends, styles and silhouettes, including its 1961 'The Slim Look' and its first men's range in the 1970s. Nothing, however, has come close to recreating the social and historical impact of that first controversial New Look from February 1947.

ICONIC STYLE
QUEEN ELIZABETH II'S CORONATION ATTIRE

Discover the ornate outfit that Elizabeth II wore to her ceremony

Cecil Beaton's photographs of the Queen on her coronation day remain among some of the most iconic royal portraits in history

Queen Elizabeth II's coronation attire

THE IMPERIAL STATE CROWN
The current state crown was made by royal jewellers Garrard & Co in 1937 for the coronation of George VI and is modelled on a crown made for Queen Victoria. The silver, gold and platinum frame is decorated with 2,868 diamonds, 273 pearls, 17 sapphires, 11 emeralds and five rubies.

THE SCEPTRE
The Sovereign's Sceptre was made for the coronation of Charles II in 1661 and represents the sovereign's temporal power at the head of the state. The 530-carat Cullinan I, the largest colourless cut diamond in the world, is mounted in the head of the sceptre.

CORONATION EARRINGS
The coronation earrings were made for Queen Victoria in 1858, using diamonds retrieved from other pieces in the royal collection such as an old Order of the Garter badge. Since 1911, they have been traditionally worn by every queen at the coronation ceremony.

CORONATION NECKLACE
Made for Queen Victoria in 1858 by Garrard & Co, the coronation necklace comprises 25 cushion diamonds with the 22.48-carat Lahore diamond as a pendant. Since 1902, it has been worn by every queen at their coronation and is one of the Queen's favourite pieces.

THE ORB
The Sovereign's Orb was made for the coronation of Charles II in 1661 and represents the Christian world. Made from solid gold and weighing 2.6 pounds, it is decorated with 375 pearls, 365 diamonds, 18 rubies, nine emeralds, nine sapphires, one amethyst and one piece of glass.

QUEEN ELIZABETH II'S ARMILLS
The Queen's solid gold ceremonial bracelets, known as armills, were a coronation gift from the Commonwealth and intended to replace the old pair, which had been in use since 1661. The bracelets represent sincerity and wisdom as well as being symbolic of the bond between the sovereign and their people.

THE ROBE OF STATE
Elizabeth II's heavy purple velvet Robe of State was specially made for her coronation by the royal robe makers Ede & Ravenscroft and follows strict guidelines which stipulate that the train should be six yards long, trimmed with ermine and decorated with gold embroidery.

THE GOWN
The Queen's white satin gown was designed by Norman Hartnell and took eight months to create, using British silk, which was painstakingly decorated with the embroidered floral emblems of Britain and the Commonwealth and then embellished with thousands of diamanté, crystals and seed pearls.

© Alamy, Getty, Julia Lillo

In 1944 a new invention captured the imagination of Western society. It wasn't a wartime technology or a new labour-saving device. It was a radical new idea, one that shifted popular culture immediately and irrevocably, and one that would transform the landscape of fashion forever. It was the concept of the teenager.

The idea of the teenage years as a distinct life stage came out of a confluence of economic growth, changes in education policy, and an end to National Service, and took effect as the 'Baby Boom' cohort of children born at the end of World War II entered their teens. Freed from the threat of compulsory military service and the economic necessity of working to contribute to the family finances, still in school or working for wages they could largely keep, and living in a world characterised by industrialised wealth and the end of rationing, this new kind of people - not children any more, not quite adults - had fewer responsibilities, more time, and more disposable cash. And they wanted to spend that money on feeling and looking good.

Traditionally children transitioning into adulthood had worn similar clothes to their parents before them. For all but the very wealthiest, trends in clothing were drawn in broad strokes - a hemline ascending here, a lapel widening there - rather than in radical seasonal upheavals. For centuries, the clothes you wore were created by either yourself and your family or, if you were wealthy enough, a tailor, dressmaker, or Paris atelier, and the amount of labour that went into them meant that they needed to last a long time to justify that investment. In the 19th century ready-to-wear clothing became available

In its early years fast fashion was still manufactured in the same country as it would be sold in, like this menswear factory in Wales, UK, 1965

"The new teenagers didn't want to dress like their parents. They wanted to dress like themselves"

for men, inspired by the bulk production of military uniforms. It took longer for womens' clothing to adopt ready-to-wear templating, and this only really happened with a shift in style from the ornate fashions of the Victorian and Edwardian eras to the sleeker silhouettes of the early 20th century. Department stores offered tailoring services to ensure customers had a perfect fit - ready-to-wear clothing was manufactured with enough material to allow for letting out, or down, waists and hems, as well as taking them in or up. Many housewives also had the skills to do this themselves, and a sewing machine was a fixture in most working and middle-class homes. The rationing mindset and 'make do and mend' ethos of World War II and its immediate aftermath was still very much in effect into the 1950s. But the new teenagers didn't want, or need, to dress like their parents. They wanted to dress like themselves.

Luckily for those teenagers, it was now possible to do that more cheaply than ever before. The Second World War had been a time of rampant industrial invention, and one of the things

FASHION GOES FAST

The postwar technologies and economy of the 1960s saw a radical reimagining of how clothing was created, and who for – but it all started with an accident...

Written by April Madden

In 1966, America's
referred to Biba as "the
cementing the brand's
fashio

Fashion goes fast

The first Hennes (now H&M) store founded in Västerås, Sweden, in 1947 by Erling Persson

Britain's 1950s Teddy Boy youth culture had a grittier, edgier image than the wholesome American fashions that inspired it

chemical companies had poured research into was synthetic fibre. Nylon had been invented in 1931 and 'artificial silk' rayon as far back as 1894, but the military need for textiles to create uniforms, parachutes, seating and more drove innovation still further.

By the 1960s most of the fibres we're familiar with today were finding their way onto the high street. Acrylic, polyester, Spandex, modal and viscose were now available, and they were cheaper, quicker and less labour-intensive to produce than cotton, linen, wool and silk. They could also be produced in large, consistent batches, ideal for bulk ready-to-wear retail.

Three key retailers would drive the rise of fast fashion, and they would go on to transform how all of us buy and wear clothes. The earliest was H&M. Founded in Västerås, Sweden, in 1947 by Erling Persson, the world's second-largest international clothing retailer started out as a single womenswear store called Hennes ('hers') before merging with a Stockholm shop called Mauritz Widforss that sold hunting apparel in 1968. H&M expanded throughout Europe in the 1960s and 70s and would go on to acquire a mail-order company called Rowells in the 1980s, which paved the way for its truly global reach. Selling their own-label H&M and Divided ranges, as well as sister brands & Other Stories, Monki, Cos, Arket and Weekday, you can find a H&M in almost every country in the world. Only one fashion retailer is bigger: Inditex. You may not have heard of this company by name, but you know their brands, which include Massimo Dutti, Stradivarius, Pull&Bear, and their founding flagship Zara. Founded by shirtmaker Amancio Ortega in A Coruña, Spain, in 1963, Zara started out replicating high-end designs for a low-cost market. Initially manufacturing in the founders' home, today Zara's fast-fashion industrial complex can get a garment from a designer's drawing board to shop floors across the globe in as little as 15 days. Neither H&M nor Zara invented the fast-fashion manufacturing model, however. The credit for that goes to a British brand that started out as a little mail-order business,

DISPOSABLE DRESSES

A quirky promotional item that sums up fast fashion

Today we worry, with good reason, about the amount of discarded mass-produced clothing that ends up in landfill, incinerated, or in notorious open-air textile dumps like the one in Chile's Atacama Desert. Back in the 1960s, however, the throwaway nature of fast fashion was what made it cool. Consumers were so used to hand-me-downs, make do and mend, and clothes built to last a lifetime, that the idea of quickly made, disposable fashion was fresh, spontaneous and exciting. And nothing was more disposable than the paper dress.

Originally conceived in 1966 as a promotional item by American company Scott Paper, the first paper dress was a gimmick designed to match another equally disposable innovation: paper plates and napkins. Priced at $1.95, the single-use party set was so popular it shifted over half a million units in its first year alone. Other companies soon saw the advertising benefits of the paper dress. Campbell's riffed off pop artist Andy Warhol's iconic screenprint of their soup cans, British airline BOAC dressed its stewardesses in colourful mini versions for a photoshoot. In 1967 a British Pathé newsreel showcased paper fashions for British tourists to take on sunsoaked package holidays, which included a mini-dress, playsuit, hat, shoes, and even a paper bikini.

The original paper dress was conceived as an advertising gimmick to promote a new range of disposable tableware for parties

117

TEENAGE KICKS

Fast fashion aimed at young people changed the way we wear clothes

Decades after her feature article for the *Daily Mirror* helped Biba to create fast fashion, journalist Felicity Green spoke to *The Lady* magazine about how Barbara Hulanicki's label, with its focus on teenage trends, had transformed the fashion landscape. "Until the 1960s, young women copied their mothers, having no choice," she explained. Biba's fresh, inspirational styles, and the dramatically lit boutique the brand opened in the wake of the gingham dress incident, transformed that, as did the advances in production time and volume brought about by Biba's unexpected success. Fast fashion was aimed squarely at the newly lucrative youth market, and this upended how older women bought clothing too. Youth fashions saturated the market, becoming more and more prevalent by the turn of the 21st century. "Now," noted Felicity Green, "nobody wants to look like an old lady, including old ladies. The middle-aged market... is having to struggle to survive." Traditionally successful retailers in this market, like Britain's Marks and Spencer, have been forced to adapt or die. Gone are the days when a woman's thirties meant swapping stylish clothes for a cardigan, midi skirt and sensible shoes – unless you're rocking a deliberately tweedy dark academia aesthetic, that is.

ABOVE Biba's popularity as a teenage hangout meant that its youthful focus soon became as important to the fashion industry as its production system

attained dizzying heights as a celebrity favourite in the swinging London of the 1960s, and then came crashing down. That brand was Biba.

Polish-born Barbara Hulanicki started her career as a fashion illustrator in the late 1950s, creating representations of ready-to-wear garments and Paris fashions for adverts and fashion magazines. Fresh out of art school herself, she knew that there were many other young women like her who didn't want to wear the staid, matronly designs she had to draw for her clients. So she decided to do something about it. In 1963, Hulanicki and her husband Stephen Fitz-Simon launched Biba's Postal Boutique (Biba was her younger sister's nickname) from their London home. The name was chosen for its cute, non-traditional sound, to reflect the fact that Biba's Postal Boutique was aimed directly at teenage girls and young women.

In its early days the business languished somewhat, but thanks to her illustration career, Hulanicki had many contacts among fashion editors. In 1964, *Daily Mirror* journalist Felicity Green was putting together a feature on young women working in the fashion industry, and as part of her article, she invited Hulanicki to create a unique item for *Mirror* readers to buy at a special price. Hulanicki readily agreed. She decided to produce something new and fun that would appeal to British girls.

In the 1950s teenage trends had been led by the USA. Postwar America's preppy collegiate look, emblematic of a burgeoning middle class and centred on smart-casual suiting and frothy circle skirts, had translated across the Atlantic into the edgier Teddy Boy style. But Teds and their flamboyant female equivalent Judies were old hat by the time Hulanicki was coming up with an idea for Felicity Green's feature. Instead, her radical design prioritised clean lines, simple shapes, and a daringly short skirt, in a fun but also crucially cheap fabric that she had some stock of. Hulanicki produced a simple sleeveless shift dress with a small cowl collar and a keyhole at the back in a fresh bright pink gingham, with a matching triangular headscarf. Cheeky and fun, its short length, simple A-line and high collar elongated and slimmed the figure and showed an unexpectedly naughty hint of skin and an inordinate amount of leg. Popular myth claims that another British designer, Mary

118

Fashion goes fast

"Teens wanted fresh new looks, they wanted them cheap, and they wanted them now"

Quant, invented the mini skirt in 1964, but in fact the dramatically shortening hemlines were a touchstone of street style across Europe in the early 60s, especially in Paris and London. The gingham print and the jaunty headscarf were a nod to the quintessentially French glamour of star Brigitte Bardot, photographed holidaying in St Tropez. The hot pink colourway meanwhile alluded to 1930s designer Elsa Schiaparelli's signature shocking pink. The Surrealist Italian designer had made the eye-popping hue a signifier not only of high fashion but of up-to-the-minute modernity. (For Schiaparelli it also symbolised Eastern exoticism, coincidentally something that would become a fascination for Biba's clientele too later in the decade.)

Biba's Postal Boutique was small enough that it sourced its raw materials from ordinary high-street fabric shops, and up until the *Daily Mirror* offer sales had been sluggish. It made its relatively poor performance into a feature rather than a bug by advertising that only 500 of each of its items would be made. The morning after the *Daily Mirror* offer was published, however, orders were at 4,000 and climbing. The dress was priced at 25 shillings, or about £25 today – easily affordable even for teenagers in the economic climate of the time. The problem was Biba's Postal Boutique didn't have the fabric to produce even a quarter of that number. Hulanicki and her husband had to think fast, and talk even faster. Phoning fabric factories across the UK, they frantically bought hundreds of bolts of pink gingham from wherever they could get it, even pushing textile mills to weave more to order. Biba became the first ready-to-wear fashion company to source cheap fabric from multiple wholesalers at once in order to fulfil a large volume of sales. Orders for the *Daily Mirror* dress set eventually topped out at over 17,000, but despite that, the fledgling company's ill-preparedness for the sheer volume of sales meant that the iconic outfit ended up making a loss.

The Biba dress debacle was the beginning of a new operating model for fashion design, manufacture and retail. It showed that customers no longer wanted to wait for designers, seamstresses and tailors to produce classic but dull garments. Teenagers in particular had neither the money or the time. They wanted fresh new looks, they wanted them cheap, and they wanted them now. In a world where synthetic fibre had revolutionised textile manufacture that was suddenly possible, and Biba's accidental upheaval of the sourcing process became the catalyst for a sudden sea change in how clothing was made, bought, and worn. The age of fast fashion had begun.

The 1960s witnessed a remarkable transformation in trends, with hemlines rising significantly

The fashions of the 1960s not only transformed what we wear, they changed how it was made too

Biba's staff channelled the aspirational fashion-forward aesthetic that the brand was known for, like this shop assistant in 1969

ICONIC STYLE
PRINCESS DIANA'S WEDDING DRESS

The secrets hidden in the seams of Diana's wedding dress

While some thought that Diana's dress was a masterpiece, others considered it messy and over the top

Princess Diana's wedding dress

SECRET DESIGN
Diana chose David and Elizabeth Emanuel to design her wedding dress, which was created in the greatest secrecy. The Emanuels even blacked out their windows to prevent anyone catching a glimpse. Fittings for the dress were complicated by the fact that Diana lost five inches from her waist before the wedding, which meant that it had to be adapted several times and she had to be sewn into it.

SEAMSTRESSES
Almost entirely handmade, Diana's silk taffeta gown featured carefully attached antique lace that used to belong to Queen Mary, as well as thousands of crystal sequins and 10,000 pearls. A second, simpler dress was also made in case the design of the first dress leaked to the press. The completed dress cost £9,000 (equivalent to about £30,000 in 2018).

FLOWERS
A traditional small bridal posy would not do as it would be dwarfed by her gown. Instead, the florist Longmans created three identical sweeping bouquets that incorporated blooms from all around the country, including – by special request of Prince Charles – the yellow 'Mountbatten' rose as well as the traditional sprig of myrtle.

WELL HEELED
Although they wouldn't be seen by many on the big day, a great deal of care was taken to make sure that Diana's wedding shoes were perfect. They were handmade by Clive Shilton using silk duchess satin dyed to match the dress and then decorated with 542 mother of pearl sequins, seed pearls, lace and heart-shaped trims. Another heart flanked by 'C' and 'D' was engraved into the soles.

VEIL
Diana's enormous train called for an even longer veil, which was held in place by the beautiful Spencer tiara. Comprising 153 yards of tulle, it proved as difficult to control as the train, as it transpired that they were too bulky to fit into Diana's carriage. The veil sparkled thanks to 10,000 sequins, all of which were sewn into place by just one lady, who worked in greatest secrecy in her sitting room.

HEIRLOOMS
Diana decided that her fairytale gown didn't need much jewellery as it was already so flamboyant, and so wore it without a necklace. She also didn't own much jewellery at the time and so borrowed a pair of diamond earrings from her mother.

SOMETHING BORROWED
Diana's 'something old' was antique lace that had belonged to her husband's great grandmother, Queen Mary; her 'something new' was her wedding ensemble; her 'something borrowed' was the Spencer tiara; and the all-important 'something blue' was a tiny ribbon bow sewn into the waistband, along with a tiny horseshoe of 18-carat yellow gold studded with diamonds.

THE TRAIN
When Diana found out that the longest royal train on record was 23-feet long, she insisted that her train should be 25 feet, which created issues for the designers as their studio wasn't big enough to accommodate it. In the end they had to make it in one of the Buckingham Palace galleries.

WHAT LIES beneath...

Jane Austen's heroines might not have worn any knickers, but centuries before anyone had even dreamed of bloomers, the Romans had different ideas. From going commando to drawers, corsets and a gentleman's linen, the history of underwear is a fascinating one

Written by Catherine Curzon

A dancer whips up her skirts to reveal her bloomers underneath

What lies beneath

I f we think of underwear as merely a means to cover one's nudity, then the earliest form must be the loincloth. Worn as both outer and underwear since ancient times, loincloths were the most rudimentary covering imaginable. However, that wasn't always the case and, 4,500 years ago in Egypt, the Badarian people refined the loincloth into something more akin to a pair of underwear, made of linen or, for menstruating women, goatskin. A little later, ancient Egyptians signalled their status through the schenti, a simple linen kilt that preserved one's modesty whilst remaining comfortable in the hot weather. Popular with deities, pharaohs and commoners alike, they were a cool option in the heat of Egypt.

The Romans were likewise no stranger to underwear and favoured the subligaculum, which came in the form of either a loincloth or a pair of simple shorts and were particularly popular with athletes and gladiators. In fact, it may come as a surprise to learn that the first bra-like garment can also be traced back to the days of ancient Greece and Rome, where women wore a bandeau-style bra known as a strophium. These garments were made of leather or linen and were tied around the chest, functioning much as a modern breast-binder does today. For the ancient people, underwear was functional rather than fancy.

ABOVE
François Boucher's 1742 painting *La Toilette* depicts two women getting dressed

LEFT
Stays were the height of fashion in the 1700s

"For those with money, the wrists would be embroidered"

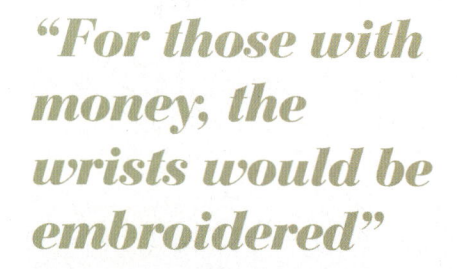

For centuries, the chemise or shift was the first layer that a woman would wear against her skin. She would then add her corsets, panniers, petticoats, or whatever else fashion demanded

By the Middle Ages, underwear had moved on far beyond the loincloth and strophium. Though items that are everyday for us were not yet worn, other types of underwear had gained popularity and these reflected the fashions that they were worn beneath. Under their gowns women worse a shift or chemise, a long linen garment that sat against the skin and was far easier to wash than the often elaborate gowns that were popular amongst the wealthy. For those with money, the neckline and wrists of these chemises would be embroidered or accessorised with lace as a sign of status and atop them women wore petticoats, or underskirts, which were also washable and helped to give the skirt a fashionable shape. Of course, women of the upper classes also wore elaborate underpinnings to shape their skirts, with more elaborate and extreme examples serving as a clear symbol of wealth and social status.

For Middle Ages men who didn't have money to throw around, a pair of loose-fitting pants named braies would be the everyday undergarment. Rather like a pair of chaps, they covered each leg to the upper thigh and tied at the waist and knee, with a

Women would wear bloomers to preserve their modesty while they cycled

flap at the top to enable the wearer to perform their intimate business without having to take the entire garment down.

For the Tudors, meanwhile, it was all about drama, and women wore farthingales, which are conical underskirts stiffened with hoops. These eventually gave way to the enormously fashionable French farthingale, which was a cartwheel-like disc that was worn around the waist. The skirt then fell from the edges of the farthingale, often giving it a vast circumference and that distinctive Tudor shape. Add a bumroll to pad the hips and you're good to go.

What we recognise as early corsetry also emerged in the 16th century, known then as "pairs of bodies". These were not intended to tightlace, but to provide support and a smooth shape to women beneath their clothes. Stiffened with whalebone, reeds or wood, depending on the budget, they would be laced around the bust and waist, to hold them firmly in place.

For the men of the 18th century, shirttails became a rudimentary nappy, so you'd better hope the men of your acquaintance could afford to change their shirts often!

Men, meanwhile, wore a shirt beneath a doublet and a pair of hose, somewhat similar to modern tights. Most noticeable in the Tudor era, however, was a piece of underwear that was very much intended to be seen: the codpiece. This was a piece of triangular cloth that was stitched into the hose at the groin, and for men with money, it became the only way to show off one's status. Men such as Henry VIII favoured oversized codpieces in rich fabrics, decorated with embroidery and precious stones. It was anything but subtle.

By the 18th century, men had cast off their codpieces and now had an even more simple option for underwear: something akin to a pair of knee-length linen drawers worn beneath their breeches. However, most men made do with the tails of their shirts, which would be pulled through between the legs from the back, then up over the groin, forming something resembling a nappy. Of course, how often one could change and launder one's shirts very much depended on each man's personal circumstances. For those with money who could purchase shirts by the dozen, keeping

What lies beneath

This 1890 photograph reveals two women getting dressed, with one tugging tightly at the other's corset laces

RIGHT This elaborate corset might be familiar to those who believe that all corsets were laced as tight as possible, but for most women that wasn't the case

their shirttails clean and free of odour was easy; it was simply something the servants did. For those with less generously stuffed wardrobes, no servants and perhaps precious little cash, however, it was a different story. It's fair to say that a man's shirttails could tell quite the story.

For women of means, meanwhile, things were getting ever more elaborate. Just like their ancestors in the Middle Ages, they wore chemise, shift and petticoat, and they also continued to dramatically shape their bodies with precision-engineered underpinnings. On top of her chemise, a woman would wear her stays, the next generation in the development of the corset. Once again these were not intended to be worn tight, nor were they supposed to create a dramatic, eyecatching shape. Instead, they were to provide support in the bust and back. Fastened by

LACES SAVE LIVES!
Few loved tightlacing as much as Empress Elisabeth of Austria

Empress Elisabeth of Austria was devoted to lacing her corsets as tightly as possible, and maintained a punishing exercise regime in an effort to keep her waist at its infamous 16 inch size. As wife of Emperor Franz Joseph I, Sisi didn't have too many demands on her time in terms of housework or other chores, let alone work, so indulging her love of custom-made corsets became her hobby of choice. She had her leather corsets made in Paris to order and wore them for only a few weeks at a time before they had to be replaced. By the age of 30, Sisi refused to be photographed, for fear of being seen to age.

In 1898, the 60-year-old empress visited Geneva, where she was attacked by an Italian anarchist named Luigi Lucheni. He struck Sisi in her breast, stabbing her with a four-inch blade; because of her tight corsets, however, the wound did not bleed and it was assumed that he had punched her. However, when the empress collapsed, she was taken to safety and made comfortable. With her corsets holding the wound closed, nobody realised how severely injured Sisi was until she failed to regain consciousness. Concerned for their mistress, Sisi's ladies-in-waiting loosened her dress and corset in an effort to make her comfortable. Instead they noticed a brown stain on her breast, where the blade had gone in. With the tight corset released, the wound haemorrhaged, killing Empress Elisabeth.

Empress Sisi was famed for her tiny waist, which she went to great extremes to maintain

125

AMELIA BLOOMER

An advocate for women's rights, Amelia Bloomer gave her name to a very particular undergarment!

Amelia Bloomer gave her name to a fashion craze that she hoped would give women a new sense of freedom

Amelia Jenks Bloomer was born in New York in 1818. She was a dedicated activist for the rights of women and the editor of *The Lily*, a newspaper that featured the works and theories of notable suffragists. It isn't this that has seen her name enter the everyday lexicon, however, but her dedication to a new direction for women's fashion.

Concerned by the restrictive clothing women wore, Bloomer promoted a new look which would be designed to meet the needs of women, rather than fashion, and would be comfortable, hygienic and allow free movement. Bloomer's dream became reality when she saw an outfit designed by Elizabeth Smith Miller, which consisted of loose trousers gathered at the ankle, worn beneath a short dress. Bloomer took to the outfit enthusiastically and promoted it in her magazine, leading her readers and followers to follow her fashionable lead.

Unsurprisingly, 1850s America did not take to this new look and scathingly dubbed the outfit the Bloomer Costume, or bloomers. Women who wore bloomers were mocked in the press and on the street for what was considered as masculine and eccentric dress, a world away from what any decent woman would wear. It's worth noting, of course, that women wearing trousers was simply unheard of and led men to accuse bloomers fans of being male impersonators. The craze eventually died out, but bloomers were back in the 1890s, worn by keen female cyclists who didn't care a jot for what men might think.

lacing, stiffened stays could be further enhanced by placing by a wooden or whalebone busk down the centre of the breast, which would help the lady's posture to remain suitably upright. Just like corsets and the Tudor pair of bodies, these would never sit against the skin, but always atop the chemise.

Though women were not yet looking to drastically reshape their upper bodies, just as the farthingale shaped the skirt, now the cage-like pannier took on that role. Panniers could be extreme, extending out from either hip for six feet or more at court occasions, but most were more subtle than that. For those who couldn't afford custom-made panniers, layers and layers of petticoats achieved something resembling the same effect. Far from showing off a lady's natural shape, which would become fashionable during the Regency, the emphasis was on exaggerating it. Of course, just like with the French farthingales of centuries earlier, panniers served another role too. The wider the pannier or farthingale, the more fabric a dress would require simply to do justice to the dramatic underpinnings, and the more fabric a dress required, the more money its owner must have.

By the Victorian era corsets had become a must-have for women of all classes. However, whilst the idea of the skinny waist and myths of rib-removal continue to fascinate, the latter is likely entirely apocryphal, whilst the former was far from the experience of most women. Rather, tight laced corsets were the preserve of a very specific niche; the vast majority of women wore their corsets laced to a comfortable degree whilst

BELOW
In some instances, panniers would be obnoxiously wide, meaning that the wearer had to pass through doorways sideways

ABOVE
By the 1920s, women's underwear had changed forever. The watchwords were freedom, comfort and fashion

What lies beneath

Four men parade around and pose in their long johns, 1915

Photographed in 1944, these draftees show off the range of underwear available to men by the middle of the 20th century

satisfying the narrow-waisted, wide-hipped fashion. As waists grew more defined, the elaborate panniers gave way to the crinoline and eventually the bustle, continuing to give gowns their shape and flow.

Perhaps most interestingly of all though, this era saw the emergence of "open drawers", long, loose-fitting pantalettes that were split at the crotch. They were perfect to wear beneath the elaborate crinoline cages and, as the 19th century turned into the 20th, the bloomer finally made its debut. Intended to give women a comfortable alternative to open drawers, they were controversial at their launch, and considered far too masculine for decent women.

Times, of course, were changing. As men's drawers continued to be a popular choice, women wanted more. The upcoming younger generation rejected the restrictive clothing of their mothers and grandmothers and wanted underclothes better suited to the new world that was dawning, where sport, pastimes, suffrage and perhaps even work beckoned. The corset shrank into something more like a girdle, with straps to attach garters, and crinolines became a thing of the past.

In 1914, a revolution hit women's underwear with the introduction of the brassiere, designed by Mary Phelps Jacob. Comfortable and easy to wear, they could be paired with modern knickers in comfortable and attractive fabrics, whilst the neck-to-toe chemise was also consigned to history, reimagined now as the slip, a much shorter garment made of a lightweight fabric.

Men, meanwhile, stuck to their drawers until the 1930s, when Cooper's launched the Jockey Y-front in 1935. In the wake of World War II, boxer shorts also became a popular choice, thanks to being part of standard issue kit to US servicemen. Just as women's underwear had modernised, so to have that for men. Long johns might still be an option for those who preferred drawers, but for the modern man there was an increasing array of options to choose from.

Once they had cast off their corsets, women never looked back. Bras developed over the decades into the infamous bullet shape of the 1950s, whilst the New Look of Christian Dior demanded a girdle to draw in the waist. However, this return to restrictive garments didn't last long as women once again

> "The younger generation rejected the restrictive clothing of their mothers"

demanded comfort, burning their bras and throwing aside their girdles. The modern era of underwear was dawning. What innovation we see today is often in fabric and fit, as underwear has become big business for designers and high street stores alike. Today, the choice is seemingly endless and it's all about looks and comfort, a far cry from panniers, bumrolls and busks.

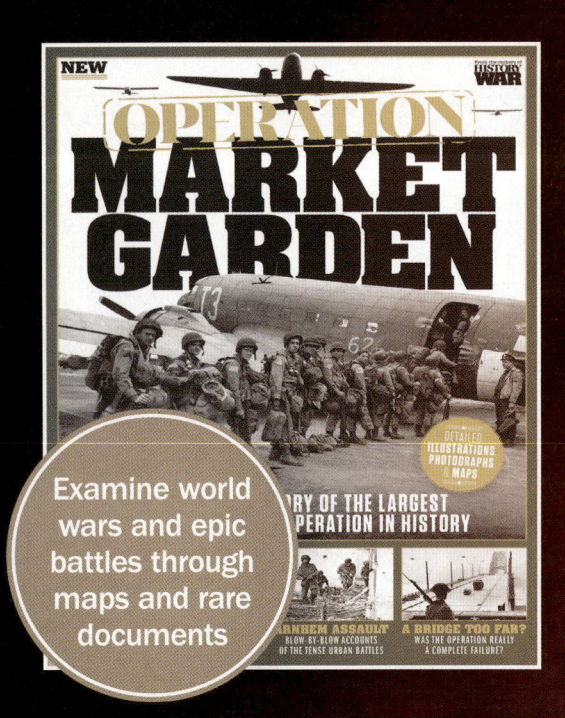

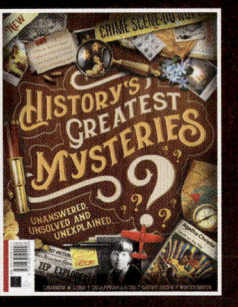

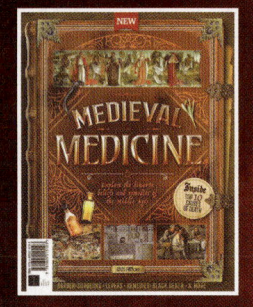

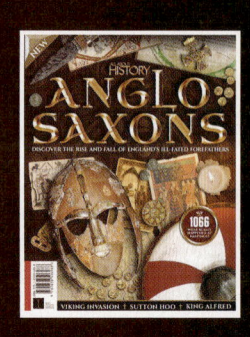

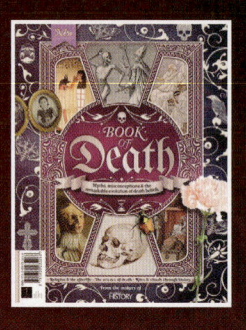

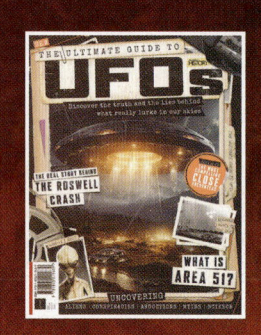

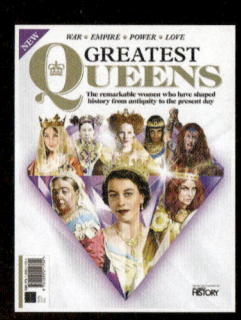

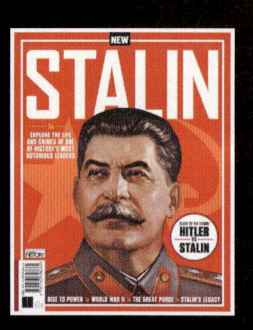

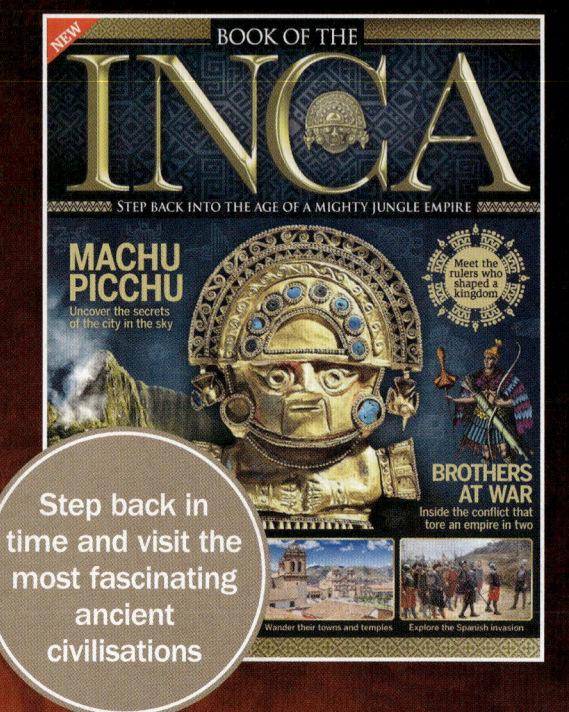

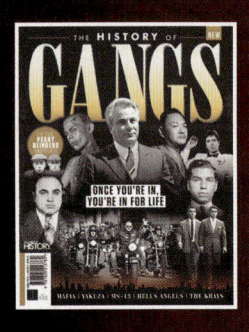

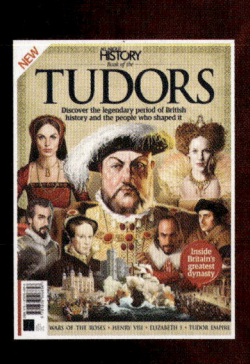

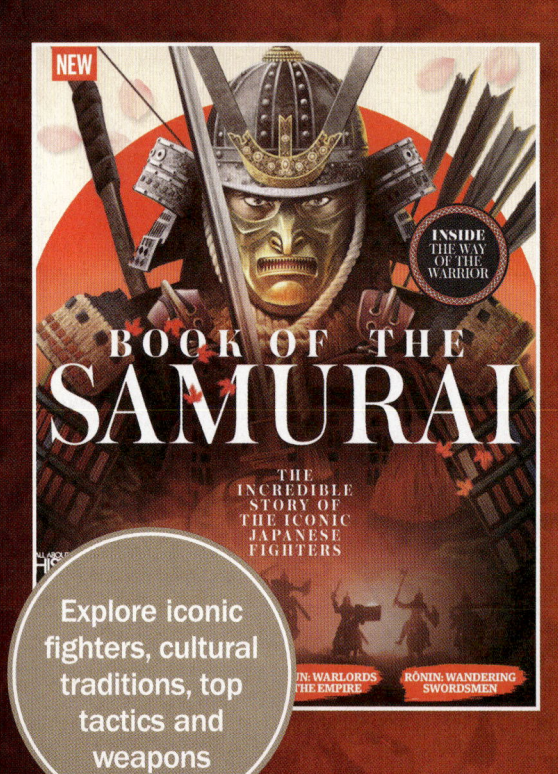

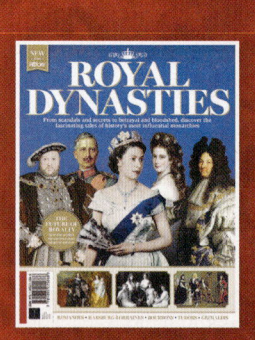

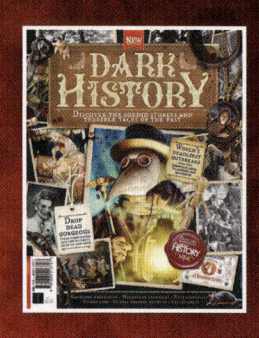

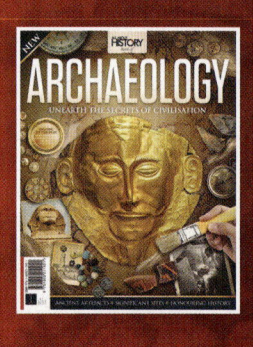

Examine world wars and epic battles through maps and rare documents

Step back in time and visit the most fascinating ancient civilisations

Explore iconic fighters, cultural traditions, top tactics and weapons

✓ Get great savings when you buy direct from us

✓ 1000s of great titles, many not available anywhere else

✓ World-wide delivery and super-safe ordering

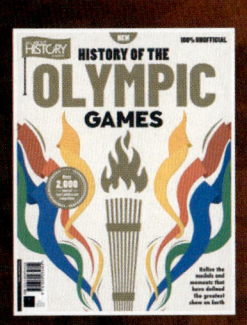

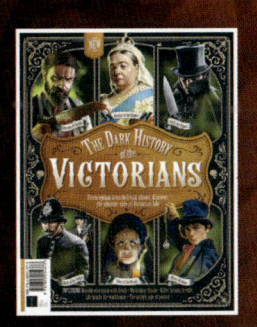

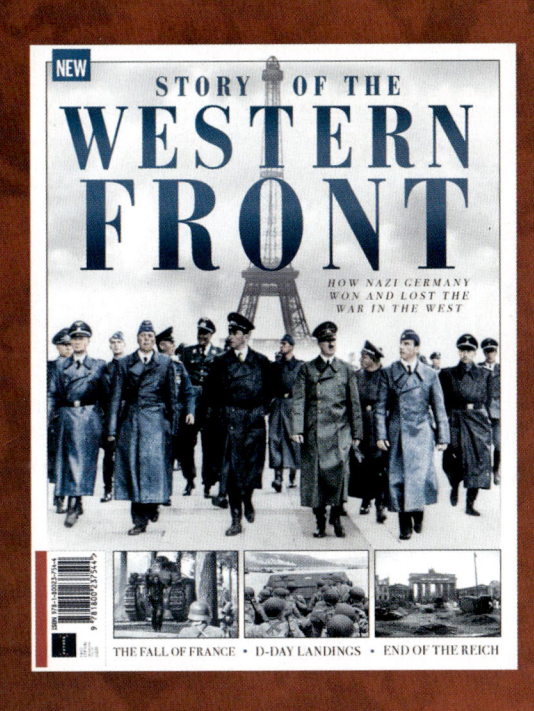

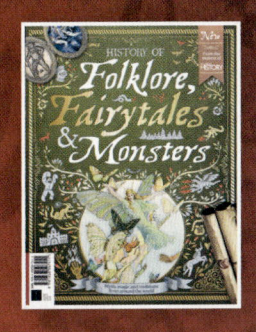

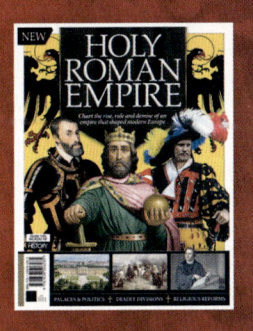

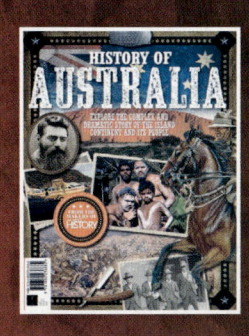

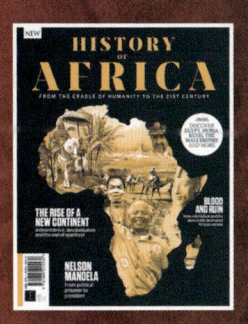

STEP BACK IN TIME WITH OUR HISTORY TITLES

Immerse yourself in a world of emperors, pioneers, conquerors and legends and discover the events that shaped humankind

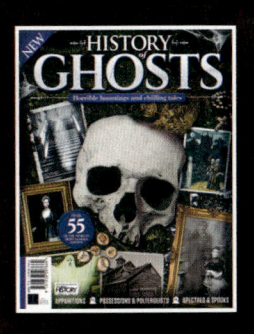

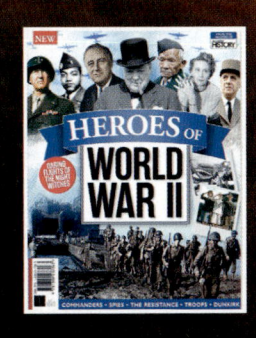

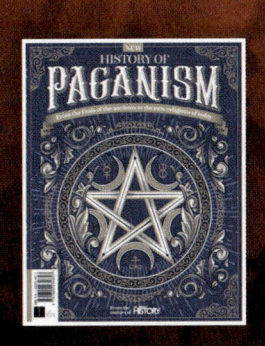

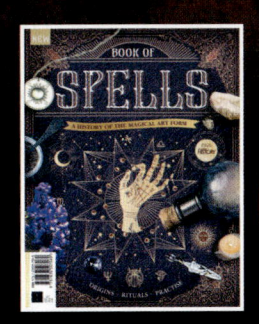

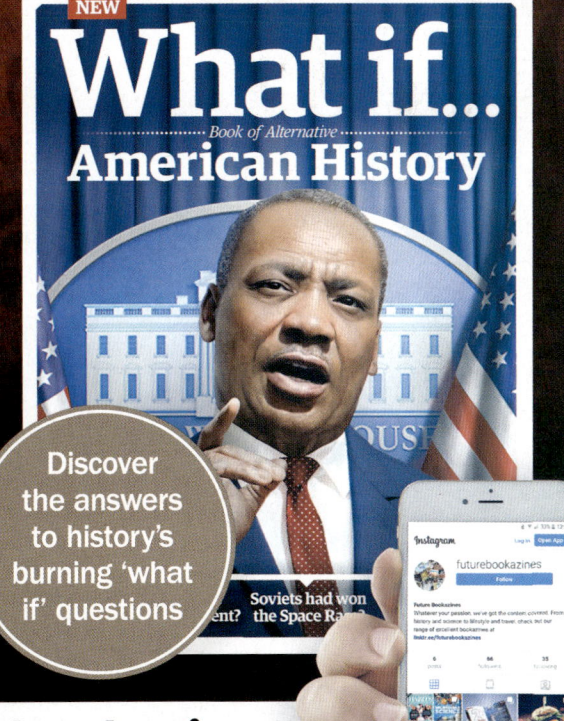

Discover the answers to history's burning 'what if' questions

Follow us on Instagram @futurebookazines

www.magazinesdirect.com
Magazines, back issues & bookazines.

FUTURE

The HISTORY of FASHION

Future PLC Quay House, The Ambury, Bath, BA1 1UA

Editorial
Group Editor **Philippa Grafton**
Senior Designer **Briony Duguid**
Head of Art & Design **Greg Whitaker**
Editorial Director **Jon White**
Managing Director **Grainne McKenna**

All About History Editorial
Editor **Jonathan Gordon**
Designer **Tom Parrett**

Contributors
Catherine Curzon, Mark Dolan, Chris Evans, Jessica Leggett, April Madden, Dan Peel, Emily Staniforth

Cover images
Alamy, Getty, Met Museum

Photography
All copyrights and trademarks are recognised and respected

Advertising
Media packs are available on request
Commercial Director **Clare Dove**

International
Head of Print Licensing **Rachel Shaw**
licensing@futurenet.com
www.futurecontenthub.com

Circulation
Head of Newstrade **Tim Mathers**

Production
Head of Production **Mark Constance**
Production Project Manager **Matthew Eglinton**
Advertising Production Manager **Joanne Crosby**
Digital Editions Controller **Jason Hudson**
Production Managers **Keely Miller, Nola Cokely, Vivienne Calvert, Fran Twentyman**

Printed in the UK

Distributed by Marketforce – www.marketforce.co.uk
For enquiries, please email: mfcommunications@futurenet.com

History of Fashion First Edition (AHB6550)
© 2024 Future Publishing Limited

We are committed to only using magazine paper which is derived from responsibly managed, certified forestry and chlorine-free manufacture. The paper in this bookazine was sourced and produced from sustainable managed forests, conforming to strict environmental and socioeconomic standards.

All contents © 2024 Future Publishing Limited or published under licence. All rights reserved. No part of this magazine may be used, stored, transmitted or reproduced in any way without the prior written permission of the publisher. Future Publishing Limited (company number 2008885) is registered in England and Wales. Registered office: Quay House, The Ambury, Bath BA1 1UA. All information contained in this publication is for information only and is, as far as we are aware, correct at the time of going to press. Future cannot accept any responsibility for errors or inaccuracies in such information. You are advised to contact manufacturers and retailers directly with regard to the price of products/services referred to in this publication. Apps and websites mentioned in this publication are not under our control. We are not responsible for their contents or any other changes or updates to them. This magazine is fully independent and not affiliated in any way with the companies mentioned herein.

FUTURE Connectors. Creators. Experience Makers.

Future plc is a public company quoted on the London Stock Exchange (symbol: FUTR)
www.futureplc.com

Chief Executive Officer **Jon Steinberg**
Non-Executive Chairman **Richard Huntingford**
Chief Financial Officer **Sharjeel Suleman**

Tel +44 (0)1225 442 244

Part of the

ALL ABOUT HISTORY
bookazine series

Widely Recycled | ipso. Regulated